UNDERDOG REVOLUTION

I hope this book serves you as guide in your pursuit of changing the world.

BPS
May 14, 2021

UNDERDOG REVOLUTION

EMPOWERING NON-OBVIOUS WINNERS
&
UNDERSERVED COMMUNITIES

PIERRE STANLEY BAPTISTE

NEW DEGREE PRESS

COPYRIGHT © 2020 PIERRE STANLEY BAPTISTE

All rights reserved.

UNDERDOG REVOLUTION

Empowering Non-Obvious Winners and Underserved Communities

ISBN

978-1-64137-556-6   Paperback
978-1-64137-557-3   Kindle Ebook
978-1-64137-558-0   Digital Ebook

This book is my gratitude to all the people who have seen in me what I did not see in myself. The ones who never gave up on me.

My mother taught me the value of sacrifice and always believed in me.

My host mother Joanne Lapinske.

Dez Lezotte, Todd Punkee, David Pierre-Louis, Moreen Tony, Dave Hartman and Jacques Joseph for giving life to my muse.

My sincere gratitude to, Dr. Eric Rasmussen, Garry Moise, Professor Eric Koester, Stephanie McKibben, Christina Jean Louis, and Tom Adamson for editing this book.

To all my greatest cheerleaders, Youseline Vital, Myrlène Mathurin, Berline Pierre, Anne-Marjorie René, Johny Junior Jean, Djenie Dorléan, Gaetan Casséus and everybody who never left my side.

CONTENTS

| | INTRODUCTION | 11 |
| | HOW TO READ THIS BOOK | 21 |

PART 1	**LEVERAGING SCARCITY**	**25**
CHAPTER 1	THE UNDERDOG EFFECT	27
CHAPTER 2	UNDERSTANDING THE BOTTOM OF THE PYRAMID	41
CHAPTER 3	LIMITATIONS OF THE TOP-DOWN INNOVATION APPROACH	53
CHAPTER 4	THE LINK BETWEEN CONSTRAINTS AND CREATIVITY	65

PART 2	**TURNING THE PYRAMID UPSIDE DOWN**	**81**
CHAPTER 5	LEVELING THE PLAYING FIELD	83
CHAPTER 6	EMPOWERING THE DAVID'S OF THE WORLD	101
CHAPTER 7	THE UNDERDOG ADVANTAGE	113
CHAPTER 8	HUMANITY AT THE CENTER OF INNOVATION	127

PART 3.	**ENACTING THE UNDERDOG REVOLUTION**	**139**
CHAPTER 9	UNLEASHING INNOVATION AT THE BOTTOM OF THE PYRAMID	141
CHAPTER 10	THE UNDERDOG BERMUDA TRIANGLE	159
CHAPTER 11	UNDERDOGS WHO ARE CHANGING THE WORLD	171
CHAPTER 12	APPLYING UNDERDOG INNOVATION	187

| CONCLUSION | MY IDEALISTIC VIEW OF THE FUTURE | 199 |
| | APPENDIX | 203 |

Compassion is aptly summed up in the Golden Rule, which asks us to look into our own hearts, discover what gives us pain, and then refuse, under any circumstance whatsoever, to inflict that pain on anybody else. Compassion can be defined, therefore, as an attitude of principled, consistent altruism.

—KAREN ARMSTRONG

INTRODUCTION

In a defining moment of trance where he felt the presence of the gods, he split the pig's throat and let blood flow into the wood cup he passed to the other slaves to drink. On the night of August 14, 1791, the Jamaican slave and voodoo priest, Dutty Boukman, convened a group of slaves in the woods of Cap-Haitian in the French colony of Saint-Domingue. Gathered around a blazing wood fire, they chanted for freedom to the drumbeat synchronized with their dance steps while the flames and cries for liberty traveled into the universe. This spiritual ceremony of voodoo called the "Ceremony of Bois Caiman" became a catalyst to create the first black independent nation in the world.

Thirteen years following that ceremony, this group of uneducated black slaves made a vow to break their chains and to be forever remembered in history as the creators of freedom for black people around the entire globe.

In the eighteenth century, the French army was conquering territories all over the world and had won almost every battle. It was the greatest army of its time, led by the general

Napoleon Bonaparte, considered the greatest commander of the eighteenth century.[1]

With only machetes, pikes, and other rudimentary tools, tied with an insurmountable will, the slaves took the riskiest bet in human history. They fought the French army against all odds—and they won. From that victory, in May 1804, they created the first black independent nation in the western hemisphere, Haiti. Critics say:

"It represents the largest slave uprising since Spartacus' unsuccessful revolt against the Roman Republic nearly 1,900 years earlier.[2] It challenged long-held European beliefs about alleged black inferiority and about enslaved persons' capacity to achieve and maintain their freedom.[3] The rebels' organizational capacity and tenacity under pressure inspired stories that shocked and frightened slave owners in the hemisphere."

The independence of Haiti is a prime example of underdogs realizing the impossible. I couldn't choose a more perfect story to introduce my book than the Haitian Revolution. It symbolizes a legend printed in every Haitian soul and people all over the world; a distant memory immortalized as a myth constantly gifting us a sense that somehow, somewhere, someday, the impossible is still achievable.

On the micro-level, many people (underdogs) are defined by their constraints and inadequacies. On a macro-level,

---

1   (HISTORY.COM EDITORS 2009)

2   (Vulliamy 2015)

3   (Kaisary 2008)

poverty and economic fragility define most emerging countries and underserved communities. The world sees an underdog as a liability—underserved communities as a heavy weight to carry instead of an untapped opportunity. The cognitive dissonance of *negativity bias* is in full effect. The lens through which these communities and individuals are viewed is distorted by everything that's wrong about them.

The current belief is that if you are poor you have little to no ability to be creative. You cannot solve problems. Therefore, you need a savior. With often good intent, international aid organizations and charity groups come to underserved communities and emerging countries with ready-made solutions. In today's world, innovation happens from the top, then spreads out to the bottom. Rich countries, Ivy League graduates, and "apparent winners" brainstorm ideas to help the people living at the bottom of the pyramid. Millions of people live at the mercy of a few on top. Their fates hang in the hands of a few smart people who have never walked in their shoes. Maybe you are asking where would we be without Albert Einstein, Nikola Tesla, and Katherine Johnson. Yes, we need our geniuses to stretch our thinking, but more importantly, we need to create an environment where more people can exploit the magic (skills, talents) already within them.

Most of us only consider the two extremes: winners and losers. If you are not a winner, then you are a loser.

Is it that simple? Is it really just black and white? Are there any gray areas in the middle we should consider?

Life is too complex to be captured in two extreme worldviews. The truth we refuse to see is often hidden in the diversity and ambiguity we refuse to sit in.

Are the following assumptions correct?

If you do not have the winner's genes, you are doomed to fail. You cannot innovate, you cannot create, you are unfruitful. Therefore, you are in need of a savior.

Deep down, you know that isn't true. Because you've seen time and time again people without the winner's genes accomplishing and being what we did not think they could be or accomplish. But if there are no sure winners, maybe there can be no sure losers.

When I was ten years old, my mother was diagnosed with severe tuberculosis. Marie Ange Jules was a teacher who devoted more than twenty years of her life to teaching first graders at the Sœur Etienne, a Catholic school in the City of Pétion-Ville, Haiti. At a stature of five feet with a slim silhouette, she's the kind of woman who can drink pain and vomit love and affection. But on a Friday evening of 2001, the gods tested her strength and courage. On that evening, I saw a white pickup truck pull in front of our house. If I remembered correctly, it was a 1996 Tacoma. On that day, they took my mom away from me and my sister for more than six months, which seemed six years. We were not allowed to visit because they did not want us to be contaminated. Growing up without a father figure, this moment left us in horrific disarray.

During those heart-wrenching months in an otherwise innocent childhood, I took care of my little sister. I braided her hair, ironed her clothes, and managed the economy my mother left for us. This experience is one of the most excruciating pains of my life—a moment in history that should have left me broken, a flicker of darkness that wavered in my life but turned my sorrows and pains into strength.

The world is an unfair place. Good things happen to bad people just as bad things happen to good people. The universe is random. Few things are under our control. My upbringing and experience are not your typical winners-get-all story. It's a story filled with humiliation, pain, failure, and inadequacy—but with a positive twist—a twist of hope for underdogs like myself all over the world.

My personal story is not a heroic one. I spent my first year of kindergarten on the same first page of the reading book *Ti Malice* because I could not read. My mom had to take me out of kindergarten to work with me at home. As a tiny kid, my classmates used to call me "little mouse." I felt insignificant, as if the world was conspiring against me. I remember praying to "GOD," whoever that was, to make me taller. After years of bullying, I could not see past the labels put on me. I remember being drafted to play in my high school basketball team after passing all the physical tests. Guess what? I never played a game; the other kids would not let me play. I was not enough. In my current life as a social entrepreneur, when I meet people for the first time, they always say, "I have heard so many great things about you, I thought you were a tall, large, and big man." Why this reference? Because we've been unconsciously trained, to associate achievers and impact makers with a set of specific physical (height, color, body), intellectual (IQ, degree), and personality traits (charisma, confidence) that are easy to identify.

We even think people who are *pretty* are smarter. A study conducted by the University of St. Andrews found people perceived as attractive are rated as having higher intelligence. In most people's minds, winners and impact makers have specific standard physical or intellectual characteristics.[4]

For the majority of my life, I have been defined by my height, size, and inability to do math. Being born in a disadvantaged family in the poorest country in the western hemisphere added to my list of "bad hands," as one would call it. I was predisposed to be a statistic and lead a mediocre life, so I am an UNDERDOG and yet still able to rise. My losses are not powerful enough to keep me from searching and reaching the potential, not yet fully explored, in me. Each of my failings, losses, and inadequacies that I've overcome are why I am here with you today.

Over the years, I have won a speech contest with broken English and a strong Haitian accent competing against native speakers. I have broken the sales record by leading more than 120 people in my sales department, and I wrote for the *Huffington Post* while living in Haiti. In the past five years, I've co-founded and launched a co-working space with only 30 percent of the budgeted funding. I've published eBooks and dozens of educational blogs in Haitian Creole (my native language), which is a first in Haiti. I took an unknown event that used to gather only 100 people and grew it into a yearly

---

4   (Talamas 2016)

rendezvous of more than 1,000 participants, sixty-four speakers, fifty-four volunteers, and fifty-one exhibitors four years later. All of this without a Master's degree, which most of my peers have in my industry. I have done what people like me should not do.

I gained my Ph.D. from life experiences, pains, and struggles. My lack taught me how to leverage scarcity. Through my life experiences, I realized there are millions of people like me without the winner's genes but who can do great things in small ways. In my quest to understand how underdogs do the impossible, I discovered communities and organizations that made it their mission to give non-obvious winners like me a chance to explore their potential not yet explored. This discovery led me to advocate for an Underdog Revolution—and this book will get it started.

Infused with inspirational stories of real individuals who are transforming the world in ways big and small, I write this book to advocate for underdog communities and individuals. I start with psychological facts on our biases about an underdog, pass through challenges and opportunities at the bottom of the pyramid, and settle on ideas on how to even the playing field for underdogs and activate the Underdog Revolution. In the next chapters, I will sail through facts and stories to back up my bold and unconventional claim:

> **The very constraints of underdogs are what makes them powerful. Characteristics perceived as disadvantages are actually what make underserved communities stronger.**

UR (Underdog Revolution) is for leaders and ordinary people who are tired of waiting for a savior to solve their problems and underserved communities, who want to find human-centered solutions to their problems by using their own skills and the resources available to them. It's also for people in the for-profit sector and non-profit organizations who want to *do* good—not just to feel good. Who want to empower. If you are an expert or interested in unleashing innovation and creativity where resources are scarce, this book will allow you to understand how people and communities with very few resources manage to create great change on a small scale.

This book is also for any individual who has ever felt out of place in this world, who feels like they don't belong. Anybody who doesn't have the winner's gene but wants to make a difference. Whatever social class, economic background, race, ethnicity, religion—if you've ever been defined by your worst behavior or someone else's perception of your inadequacy, this book is for you. I've compiled a list of stories from underdogs all over the world who changed their immediate environment in ways that can embolden you to dig deeper into your unexplored potential.

Underdog Revolution is a book for decision-makers to reconsider where and how they allocate funding and resources when it comes to creating solutions for the bottom of the pyramid.

My hope is that this book will be a conversation starter, a stimulus for the world of innovation and social change to reconsider the way they view innovation, and a manifesto for underdogs who want to get inspired to come up with the next breakthrough ideas that will move the human race forward.

UR will help you:

- Discover the secrets behind some of the greatest revolutions carried out by the underdogs of the world.

- Understand the link between constraints and creativity.

- Understand how to enable innovation at the bottom of the pyramid.

- Learn about new models of innovation and social change that put humanity first.

- Empower you to apply the Underdog Revolution in your community, school, business, and home.

Writing this book has been one of the greatest challenges of my career. I am reviewing this introduction, sitting in the dark, and a tropical night's wind is slowly kissing my face. My two red Trojan batteries have died, and my anxiety is through the roof as the publication deadline is approaching. Haiti has been on lockdown for almost two weeks. Radio propaganda, marches, and burning tires are everywhere. Most people are staying inside fearing for their precious lives. My sanity is not always mine in a country like Haiti. While I am fighting to regain clarity of mind, I must also continue on my quest to write this book.

I used to think something was wrong with me until I stumbled upon other underdogs who feel the same way. To survive in a world built for apparent winners, I had to develop creative problem-solving skills that allowed me to differentiate myself from my peers and come up with creative solutions that require little-to-no resources. Where my talents cannot get me, my effort and work ethic can.

As I became more influential and started conquering more territories, I was desperate to understand why the world rallies behind the winners and why some of us are written off before given a chance. People called me the Maestro because I excel at recognizing ignored individuals with potential not yet explored. My inner circle is made of underdogs who are squeezing every ounce of goodness out of the opportunity life presents to them.

As George Orwell, author of *Animal Farm*, once stated:

"Writing a book is a horrible, exhausting struggle, like a long bout with some painful illness. One would never undertake such a thing if one were not driven on by some demon whom one can neither resist nor understand."

I am undertaking this project driven by one demon I cannot resist: to empower underdogs to destroy the image of the perfect and enable the performance of the impossible.[5]

---

5   (Manko 2013)

HOW TO READ THIS BOOK

Underdog Revolution (UR) is an essay on the power of underdogs and what the world can do to empower them. The book is divided into three parts, following the three-act structure used in narrative fiction. The Controlling Idea or theme states: *The constraints of underdogs are the very things that make them powerful. What is perceived as disadvantages are actually what enables underdogs to innovate and move the human race forward.*

UR is divided into three parts and each part has five elements which are combined in four chapters each. Each chapter has an average of 3000 words.

- Inciting Incident: A story that lays the groundwork for the chapters to come

- Complication: A myth or challenge that needs to be addressed to allow the Underdog Revolution to happen.

- Crisis: Explaining why the current approach we are using is wrong.

- Climax: The principles on which the book is written; the tools and models that can lead to the Underdog Revolution.

- Resolution: The advantages of the Underdog Revolution and the advantages the underdogs themselves have compared to the world.

This book is not a how-to book, nor an academic and know-it-all essay. *Underdog Revolution* is a non-fiction book that combines scientific data, philosophy, and stories. There are three ways you can read this book.

If you are thinking logically, read all the chapters in order from the intro to the conclusion. This way, I lay out the arguments, economic facts, and other elements that give the reader an understanding of why an Underdog Revolution is needed.

If you are a change-maker or leader looking for insights and model to continue your work, I recommend you start with Chapter 4 in Part One, Chapter 8 in Part Two, Chapter 12 in Part Three, and then continue reading the other chapters in order.

The third option is to start with Part Three, followed by Parts One and Two. That way you start with the elements you need to get inspired to enact the Underdog Revolution or get excited to be an ally.

This book is not meant to be accusatory. I highly encourage any reader to not take the arguments personally and see it more in a systematic way. This is not a way to throw away all the tremendous effort and work that a lot of organizations and individuals have done to make this world a better place. It's simply an accurate picture of what I've witnessed and learned from my two years of experience in the United States and twenty-eight years of experience in Haiti. I don't pretend to know everything or have all the solutions. This book is my attempt at reaching out to the world to say: *Hey! There is a group of people over here who could change the world. So stop ignoring them.*"

This is an open source book that calls for other ideas to help refine the models or stories or experiences and reinforce what is said. Social change and innovation are often being explained from the perspective of the ones at the top. This time, I think it makes sense that I use my voice for the people I represent. It would have been selfish to live my little life and enjoy blessings while knowing there are other people like me who will never have the chance to rise to their ambitions. Not because they don't have potential but because they are not seen.

PART ONE

LEVERAGING SCARCITY

CHAPTER ONE

THE UNDERDOG EFFECT

―――

The fact of being an underdog changes people in ways that we often fail to appreciate. It opens doors and creates opportunities and enlightens and permits things that might otherwise have seemed unthinkable.

― MALCOLM GLADWELL

In school, attention is paid to the smartest students. Well, the ones with perfect scores; the ones who always raise their hands and have answers to all the questions. Students with winners' genes get the most attention while the ones with unexplored potential are ignored.

When underdogs fail, they are laughed at and reminded of their inadequacies. They feel the world is rigged against them. Realizing they cannot bring value to the world around them, they shut their mouths and stop talking. They start believing that they are inadequate and begin to identify with the label others put on them. The school systems don't measure effort and character. Appreciation and respect are given based on IQ and grades with little attention to all other aspects that make a good human being or that could possibly lead you to become one.

They can't see the potential not yet explored in underdogs. The current social system only measures who they are now and cannot see what they could become, as it is in this iconic story from the Christian tradition.

For forty straight days, a powerful Philistine man, nine feet tall, came to the battle line to make fun of the Israelites and their god. This giant named Goliath inspired shaking fear, and no man had the guts to stand up to him—until the least powerful man of all decided to face him. During that time, David was visiting the army to bring news back to his village. Armed with unwavering faith, David decided to face the feared and revered soldier Goliath, who no other Israelites had the courage to face. In 1 Samuel 17, this glorious story is told in the Bible as follows:

"As the Philistine moved closer to attack him, David ran quickly toward the battle line to meet him. Reaching into his bag and taking out a stone, he slung it and struck the Philistine on the forehead. The stone sank into his forehead, and he fell face down on the ground. So David triumphed over the Philistine with a sling and a stone; without a sword in his hand, he struck down the Philistine and killed him. David ran and stood over him. He took hold of the Philistine's sword and drew it from the sheath. After he killed him, he cut off his head with the sword." [6]

While this iconic story belongs to the Christian tradition, it has been echoed across religions and societies all over

---

6   (17 n.d.)

the world. The *David versus Goliath* story in the Christian tradition has become the hallmark of the underdog. This is often the story we use to convey the extraordinary power hidden in underdogs. Little David defeated the top-dog by playing on his own strengths and acknowledging his weaknesses, which were his small size and his inability to fight with a sword. David exemplified the classic definition of an underdog as defined by the *Cambridge Dictionary*: "a person or group of people with less power, money, etc. than the rest of society."

According to the *Times of India*, the term underdog surfaced in the nineteenth century. The word originated from dogs fighting, in which the losing dog would roll over his back and allow the tougher dog to tower over him. Hence the combination of "under" and "dog" to create "underdog."[7]

For the purpose of this book, we will define underdog as an individual or group with disadvantages, few resources or unfavorable circumstances, compared to another group or individual perceived as an apparent winner. This winner possesses more likelihood for success, more assets, and a favorable environment. While the underdog knows her limitations and operates in an environment where resources are scarce, she can manage to stretch her imagination and look for unconventional methods to create the change she seeks to make and overcome the Goliaths of this world.

---

7 (Gupta 2014)

UNDERDOG EFFECT

The classic movie *Rocky* came out in 1976. With a budget of $1.5 million, it grossed $225 million in global box office receipts and became the highest-grossing film of the year.[8] Since it came out, it has had seven sequels—the last one in 2018. *Rocky* was nominated for ten Oscars and won three of them. *Rocky* holds a 93 percent "Certified Fresh" rating on Rotten Tomatoes. Critics called it a classic, the greatest sports film ever made.[9] People all over the world love it. Why does a movie hold such power in our psyche? Is it because we see ourselves in Rocky, the underdog in the movie?

I don't have scientific evidence on why a movie like *Rocky* became an inspiring stimulus in our collective psyche. One thing I know is that this is a poignant story that transcends cultures, countries, and languages. Stories of Jesus, Martin Luther King, Jr., Mahatma Gandhi, Abraham Lincoln, Nelson Mandela, Lumane Casimir, Barack Obama, Steven Pressfield, and Oprah Winfrey have the same effect on us. They compel us to stretch our imagination and evoke compassion in seeing the unfavorable accomplishing the impossible. More often than not, we gravitate toward the underdogs, we cheer them on, and we want them to beat the giant. Why do we cheer for underdogs when we know their likelihood of success is thin? I could not stop asking myself why, so I decided to find out.

Why do people support individuals and groups at a competitive advantage? When does the world side with the

---

8 (ELLER 2019)

9 (Barber 2016)

potential losers? Is there any scientific evidence to demystify this phenomenon?

There's limited evidence to assume people will favor underdogs more than the giant. The various ways of defining "underdog" are the main reason for this lack of evidence because we don't define underdogs the same way in every context. Our definition may vary depending on the situation and information we might have regarding the two different entities (underdog and top-dog). For instance, if you take two teams, one with minimal advantages and few resources and another one with a lot of resources that have been losing for the past five years, people tend to identify the former as an underdog because of its past failures. Instead of defining underdog based on lack of resources, lack of funding, and inadequacies, we also label underdogs as those with past failures even when they have the resources and talents to win.

SOCIAL IDENTITY THEORY
Winners are guaranteed to win in a world that won't take a chance on underdogs. As a matter of fact, people like to associate themselves with social groups that have a proven track record. Again and again, people want to invest their hope and emotional resources where the opportunity to win is crystal clear. This is a phenomenon called "social identity theory."[10]

Henri Tajfel, a Polish social psychologist, developed social identity theory to explain that people are motivated to support the group that boosts their self-esteem. They derive their

---
10 (Ellemers n.d.)

sense of importance from the group they support, whether it means their religion, political candidates, or soccer team. At the base of social identity theory, we find three psychological processes: social categorization, social comparison, and social identification.

Social categorization is the tendency for people to view themselves in terms of a social group instead of unique individuals.[11] In this particular instance, the group's label defines the individual. The social comparison takes place when people measure the value of a group by relatively comparing it to another group[12]. For instance, a call center agent may be seen lower in status than a soccer player and a soccer player lower in status than a politician. We rank the perceived value of others based on the social group to which they belong.

The third element of social identity theory is social identification,[13] which is the tendency for an individual to derive his or her sense of self based on the way he or she views other individuals and groups around them. In other words, we look up to others to measure our value as an individual. Therefore, an individual's social identity is a result of social categorization, social comparison, and social identification. Taking into account this social theory, we can assume that supporting a potential loser doesn't help an individual see themselves as more valuable than when supporting a potential winner. There's more emotional gain associated with a

---

11 (Study.com n.d.)
12 (Psychology Today n.d.)
13 (McLeod 2019)

winner than a loser. Let's explore more scientific evidence of why we don't support underdogs.

CORFING

CORFing, or Cutting Off Reflected Failure, the opposite of social identity theory, is the effect of distancing yourself from a losing team or group to prevent others from judging you in an unfavorable light.[14] Once again, the underdog is at a disadvantage. It's fair to deduce that people would not take a stand for the underdog (the vulnerable), even when they support them internally because of the fear of also appearing like a failure or being identified with this specific, losing, group.

The ego is at the center of our lives. We take care of our appearance, social status, and social circles to avoid being on the receiving end of negative opinions. It makes clear sense that we would want to distance ourselves from what puts our ego in jeopardy. We don't want to tarnish our reputations or be seen as a loser by association. This explains why people on social media repost good news about someone when they are making strides and ignore the same person when they are in big trouble. People's opinions and the fear of judgment weighs heavy on our emotional scale and affects the way we view ourselves, hence supporting underdogs. It's not a secret why most soccer fans support the Brazilian team—the winning chance is higher based on past success. Supporting a loser and non-apparent winner make people also look at us as losers.

---

14 (Posten 1998)

WHY WE SUPPORT UNDERDOGS

According to a 2005 study called "The Underdog Effect: Definition, limitations, and motivations. Why do we support those at a competitive disadvantage?" published by Nadav Goldschmid of the University of South Florida, there are a few scientific reasons that can explain why people root for or don't root for the underdog. Anecdotal evidence reveals that most people are willing to align with underdogs under specific circumstances, a phenomenon called the "underdog effect."[15] Let's take a look at some of these instances.

SCHADENFREUDE

Schadenfreude is in effect when someone's bad luck secretly makes you feel good. According to this theory, people tend to enjoy a powerful individual's or group's demise. In this situation, people who support underdogs are not just supporting underdogs because they like them or want them to win; they are using the underdogs as a proxy to celebrate the demise of the giant.[16]

Friedrich Nietzsche was the first to label the concept of schadenfreude as one of our emotional reactions as humans. He described it as the malicious pleasure people take in another's misfortune. We should also mention that according to psychologist Fritz Heider, people who experience schadenfreude don't actively seek the demise of other people but feel elated when they learn about a setback someone else suffered.

---

15 (Goldschmied 2005)
16 Ibid

Therefore, schadenfreude is opportunistic by nature; indirect and passive.

JUSTICE BASED-MOTIVATION

People believe the world is an unfair place. To rid the world of evil and injustice, they show a preference for the underdogs. This is particularly true when they are aware of the lack of support, inadequacies, and losses of the underdogs. We don't want to be the ones responsible for continuing to widen the divide between the winners and losers or the gap between rich and poor.[17] Our sense of justice compels us to act, to balance the world, a psychological theory called "distributive justice."

Distributive justice is a theory that advocates for radical equality. It says that each and every one of us should have the same level of material goods (including burdens) and services. Therefore, an equal amount of input should provide every individual with the same potential for output. When there's a discrepancy in the output of an underdog compared to a top-dog, even when the input and effort is the same, distributive justice is absent.[18]

We also need to point out that if people think the underdog's history of losing stems from a lack of effort, mismanagement of resources, or ineptitude, the chance for them to support the underdog drops significantly.[19]

---

17 Ibid
18 (Study.com n.d.)
19 (Goldschmied 2005)

UTILITARIAN-BASED MOTIVATION
The other basis for people to support the underdog is the opposite of schadenfreude. Rather than balancing the world and making justice for underdogs, people are driven by utilitarian motives.

From a logical standpoint, people who follow a rational thought process look at the candidates or the entities playing to see which side will give them the biggest emotional payoff. If winning is important to them, they will support the team that can win because the winners will deliver them a victory, which creates a sense of satisfaction, a sense of importance, or a sense of being part of something greater.

On the other side, they can also support the underdog knowing they have nothing to lose on an emotional level. They already expect the underdog to lose so there will be nothing to be disappointed about. Either way, they look for that emotional reassurance. In this scenario, they will have nothing to lose because they expect underdogs to fail; whereas if the team they were rooting for had the possibility to win, the emotional payoff would go into the negatives because they would have hoped to win. In this case, an expected disappointment becomes better than an unexpected loss.

HOW THE WORLD EMPOWERS WINNERS?
We live in a world that despises mistakes. We expect underdogs to perform at the same level as the giants in a society created for the winners. The environment and the resources are set in a way to be more favorable to winners. Without readjustment, winners take all. In a world that praises

perfection—that elevates the individual with a perfect score, a perfect demeanor, and perfect bodies—what opportunities are left for the imperfect? The ones who would never be perfect? Underdogs are far from perfect. They cannot reach that world-standard perfection metric we have created. What should they do?

In the entrepreneurial world, venture capitalists and investors are looking for the next Steve Jobs or Mark Zuckerberg. While these individuals have done great things for humanity, they are not the norm, and at some point, many of them were underdogs. The characteristics of the typical winner have blinded investors from seeing the potential in other entrepreneurs who have enormous opportunities to bring them. I remember reading how James Proud, founder of Hello Inc., had everything that makes a great entrepreneur. He was arrogant, sure of himself, and had the backing of Peter Thiel, but this did not prevent his company from failing massively just months after giving the double-middle-finger when asked about competition from giants like Google, Apple, and Amazon. It's a myth to think we can predict the future or decide which individual is going to make it. In 2000, Tom Brady (the best quarterback in the NFL today) was the 199th overall pick in the NFL Draft. If we keep seeking out the typical winners, we will continue to have difficulty seeing the diamond in the rough.

FIXED MINDSET

In her now-famous book *Mindset*, Carol Dweck introduced the world to the two mindsets that govern our lives: fixed and growth.

People with a *fixed* mindset believe that we are born with a certain number of skills and our characteristics are carved in stone. Meaning some of us are born with the right genes and other circumstances that guarantee success. However, the *growth* mindset theory suggests that we have undetermined potential and that effort matters in making that potential actual.[20] We can grow and become better if we put in the work and effort necessary. Our brain plasticity allows us to reinvent ourselves, learn and unlearn.[21] The adaptability factor is ingrained into our DNA, that's why we are the species currently at the top of the ladder.

Taking into account my own experiences and observations of the world around me, I suspect the fixed mindset worldview is one of the reasons why the world doesn't support underdogs. We do not believe they have what it takes to become better and change their lives. We cannot see past their raw nature because of our view that the world is either you have "it" or you don't.

After the New England Patriots drafted Tom Brady, the coach explained the thinking behind the decision: *"It's not that we said we wanted to draft a tall, lanky quarterback that ran a 5.3 [time in the] 40 [yard dash]. Those weren't the traits we were looking for,"* current Bucs general manager and then-member of the Patriots personnel staff Jason Licht said at a press conference before the 2014 season. *"But we were looking for the mental makeup ... Belichick did a lot of homework on him, along with our staff, on his mental makeup. Watching the tape,*

---

20   (POPOVA 2014)

21   (University of California Television (UCTV) 2018)

he was the guy that would go in and lead [the University of Michigan] back to victory." ²²

Not unlike a gambler who believes in luck, I believe the law of averages often plays in favor of the underdog. Every loss, every failure moves them closer to a win. The willingness to gamble with their potential without guarantees creates brave and bold leaders, entrepreneurs, and change-makers who surprise the world, inspire other underdogs, and enact powerful change like the Haitian revolution.

CONCLUSION

Having gone through to the extent of why we support underdogs, you might agree with me that the underdog bias is often unconscious. There is very little conscious effort put into supporting underdogs. I am not sure we know when we are in the presence of an underdog. What if we could identify the underdogs? What if schools, churches, and colleges did not let the underdog bias impact their decisions unconsciously?

We must bring the underdogs to the forefront of our minds when making decisions and assigning roles. Supporting or not supporting underdogs should not be left to our unconscious biases to decide; it needs to become a natural part of the equation. How many of your friends are underdogs? How many of your employees are underdogs? How many of your students are underdogs?

---

22   (Gaines 2019)

Remember, in every social setting you inhabit, there will be a community of underdogs—a group of people with disadvantages and they get ignored. It's on you now to call them in, recognize the fire in their eyes, and give them the opportunity to lead. Maybe you are asking how you will recognize them. In Chapter 7, I talk about some characteristics that can help you recognize the underdogs. Please do not just play the game with the apparent winners.

We need you as an ally. We're not asking you to stop supporting your winners. We are asking you to acknowledge us—to see us for what we can be, not just what we are not. The next Tom Brady might be in your classroom.

CHAPTER TWO

UNDERSTANDING THE BOTTOM OF THE PYRAMID

If we stop thinking of the poor as victims or as a burden and start recognizing them as resilient and creative entrepreneurs and value-conscious consumers, a new world and opportunity will open up.

— C. K. PRAHALAD, THE FORTUNE AT THE BOTTOM OF THE PYRAMID

The challenges at the bottom of the pyramid are a carefully disguised box of gold on which the world sits but won't take the time to dig deeper to find the treasure. We cannot pretend to change something we do not understand. In our quest to empower the bottom of the pyramid, it's essential to understand the people living at the bottom of the pyramid from an economical point of view and, more importantly, the mindset and aspiration that governs their lives.

When we look at the economic pyramid of the world, the bottom of the pyramid (BOP) refers to two-thirds of this pyramid as defined by Brittanica.com. The BOP represents more than 2.7 billion people living on less than $2.50 a day[23] and more than 700 million people, or 10 percent of the world population, who still live in extreme poverty, surviving on less than $1.90 a day. As of 2018, roughly 55 percent of the world's population has no access to social protection; having a job does not guarantee a decent living.[24] The bottom of the pyramid has its fair share of challenges. This abject group of seemingly poor people represents an issue for the world. A nightmare we want to wake up from that keeps replaying in our minds even when we wake up. The BOP is a painful truth that we refuse to deal with or we don't know how to deal with. As is taught in many spiritual traditions, only when we accept our painful truth and reality can we begin to change it.

LET THE NUMBERS SPEAK

In the Sustainable Development Goals that were implemented by more than 190 countries in 2015, the number one sustainable goal is to eradicate abject poverty by 2030. Ten years away from the deadline, what's the progress? Are we on track to meet this goal? While the poverty rate is at its lowest point, Jim Yong Kim, the President of the World Bank Group, doesn't think we are going to get there. He proposes one element of the solution, which we also focus on throughout the book: *"If we are going to end poverty by 2030, we need much more investment, particularly in building human capital, to help promote*

---

23   (Malik 2014)

24   (United Nations n.d.)

the inclusive growth it will take to reach the remaining poor."[25] We need to build people before building infrastructure; they are the greatest asset of the BOP.

In the developing world, more than one-third of the urban population lives in slums. They flock to the main cities from rural areas to access services non-existent in their villages. By 2025, around 100 cities will have more than 1,000,000 people.[26] The metropolitan area of Port-au-Prince, Haiti, already has a growing population of 2,618,894 (2015 estimate), according to the *Institut Haïtien de Statistique et d'Informatique* (IHSI).[27] Creating conditions for people living in rural areas to have a decent life stems from a problem of distribution and value chain.

How do we get medicine, food, training, and products to the most vulnerable living on the far side of four mountains? The problem of distribution is an impediment to any entity wanting to improve the quality of life for people living at the BOP. Whether that means physical infrastructures such as roads, trains, postal systems, value chain, or communication infrastructures, these services are not accessible for most of those at the bottom of the pyramid.

While this seems like a major challenge, it also represents a massive opportunity for international and local corporations and public-private partnerships to create adequate services and products capable of connecting the ones in need with the

---

25 (Elks 2018)
26 (Robert Muggah 2018)
27 (World Population Review n.d.)

ones capable of solving those needs. This automatically creates a new market, where people at the BOP can build a new kind of wealth. It can create great profits for these corporations.

TECHNOLOGY

According to Analysys Mason, a global consulting and research firm specializing in telecoms, mobile retail revenue will continue to increase in Sub-Saharan Africa (SSA) over the next five years and will reach $40.3 billion in 2024, despite regulatory and macroeconomic challenges.[28]

The Global System for Mobile Communications Association (GSMA) predicts that 80 percent of the 800 million people in Sub-Saharan Africa will have a mobile device by 2020,[29] which also means that many people will get access to mobile banking and technological solutions to their daily problems. Mobile penetration is projected to reach 74 percent in the Caribbean by 2025.[30] The number of internet users in Haiti has increased from 5.4 percent in 2004 to 32.5 percent in 2018, growing at an average annual rate of 17.83 percent.[31]

If these trends continue, we will assume the tech industry (if we build one) will play an important role in enabling innovation at the bottom of the pyramid. As more people get access to the internet and other tech tools, we can expect large-scale

---

28 (Analysys Mason 2019)
29 (GSMA 2018)
30 (Belinda Baah 2018)
31 (Knoema n.d.)

innovation in education, financial services, health, and other sectors that can be built on top of the internet.

We need to also mention that failed access to electricity is an existential threat to many industries in emerging countries, making it more difficult for these countries to adopt new technology in education, health, and other sectors.

ASPIRATIONS OF PEOPLE AT THE BOTTOM
There is a big myth we need to put to bed today called "poverty aspiration."[32] Many people and scholars associate poverty with the lack of aspirations of an individual. As someone who's been poor and who's still trying to get out of poverty, I want to say this is bullshit. Aspirations are not missing in the BOP. The parents spending ten hours a day selling recycled scraps from a landfill have good dreams for their children. The youth population has transformative aspirations for their lives and constantly plan how they will support their parents when they reach their social, intellectual, or financial goals. But the question remains, is the playing field even enough for these aspirations to take root, even flourish? People at the BOP can work as hard as they can, or "smarter" if you want to be philosophical, but they will never reach their goals if the system is designed in a way that prevents them from doing so. The Bermuda Triangle, which I discuss in Chapter 10, will kill each ounce of effort they will make.

The second lazy assumption is that people living at the bottom of the pyramid don't care about brands. In light of this,

---
32   (Treanor 2017)

brands targeting this market don't focus on making products aspirational. It becomes a simple commodity that doesn't provoke or satisfy emotional needs. I think it's not a good strategy because every human being aspires to be better in some regard, to move up the ladder and tell a better story about themselves. Brands hold great power, the ability to help people see themselves in a different light, a positive one. It's not enough to sell the product—the way you sell it *matters* at the BOP. If, when selling at the BOP, human dignity or human emotions are not taken into consideration, it's disrespectful for the people. They say in Haiti, "*Malere pa chen*" —"Just because I am poor doesn't mean you need to treat me poorly."

The "aspirations scarcity" in the BOP is a myth. I have sat with students, teachers, religious leaders, and street sellers, and every group I meet marvel at a future where they can realize their fullest potential.

BUREAUCRACY AND CORRUPTION
Registering a business takes ninety-seven days in Haiti, forty-two days in Honduras, 230 in Venezuela, and seventy in Somalia compared to four in Rwanda or one in New Zealand.[33] Local governments are riddled with inefficiency in many developing countries, making it difficult for the ones at the bottom to get insurance, a loan, and other essential services needed to live a decent life. If people are unable to even access basic services due to the immense bureaucracy existing in private business and local governments, there won't be an increase in the quality of life. The system designed to

---

33 (World Economic Forum 2019)

serve them is keeping them from stepping up in individual and community growth.

Corruption thrives in many poor countries because of the population's vulnerability and the fear of not having enough. Imagine your daily income depends on what you generate that day. Corruption becomes the easiest avenue for you take. Global Prosperity Lead at the *Clayton Christensen Institute* and co-author of *Prosperity Paradox* Efosa Ojomo show through data that the best way to fight corruption is to create innovation that benefits the BOP because in many of these countries, corruption is simply a way around for normal individuals navigating a broken system and for those in power to manage their insecurity.[34]

According to a Transparency International survey, 76 percent of people in the United States think political parties are corrupt, which is a similar percentage of people who hold the same belief in Romania, Ghana, Pakistan, or the Democratic Republic of the Congo. This is to say, while corruption is destructive to the BOP, we cannot solely blame poverty on corruption.[35]

POLITICAL INSTABILITY

In 2019 alone, I have spent more than seventy days at home on normal weekdays, which represents 19 percent of my year not counting weekends. Political rivalries don't just stop at tweets, TV appearances, and smear campaigns. Political unrest has

---

34 (Clayton Christensen 2019)
35 (Kenny 2017)

become the hallmark of many countries that are trying to eradicate poverty. At the moment of writing this paragraph, many businesses, hotels, and other institutions are closing their doors in Haiti. Economic activity is slowly dying because the ones in power don't deliver what they had promised to the majority. I have at least two friends who had their business vandalized or who have lost everything they have built over years in a matter of minutes. How can we motivate or inspire the younger generation to create when they've witnessed political instability destroy twenty years of work in twenty minutes?

"To date, almost every country in Africa is still haunted by historical injustices and oppressive structures that were bequeathed to the post-colonial leadership. This is institutions of the state, flawed legislative systems, and constant struggles for a political power to the detriment of the well-being of many nations, which could have moved on a path of development as part of modern societies. While the international community, whose geo-security and resource interests seem to benefit from the status quo in Africa, has not been pro- the establishment of functioning systems in Africa, instead, their involvement, continues to undermine Africa's stability through the militarization of conflicts for accumulative purposes," says the study "Political instability in Africa: Where the problem lies and alternative perspectives" published by Antony Otieno Ong'ayo of Erasmus University in the Netherlands.[36]

Governments fund gangs to withhold power. Other political groups work to use the most vulnerable people at the BOP as a human shield to remove a government from office, hence

---

36 (Ong'ayo 2008)

pushing those governments to commit crimes. You might be saying that's good, we need a revolution. Indeed, we need a revolution, but most of these movements are *not* in the interest of the population. They are rarely about improving the well-being of the people. It is most often a fight for power. A fight to know which group will have the ability to waste resources and get rich on the backs of the people. If politics (meaning "the things concerning the state") don't solve the problem of the people, it's fair to say we need a new form of politics that is working *for* the people and not to the detriment of them. I stay convinced that the political system cannot be the same in the least developed countries and the rich countries because the landscape is widely different. Call me an idealist, but I believe we need a new form of government that is supported by, and accountable to, the people and not the other way around. The population should play a larger role in the government's actions, whatever form that might take.

OPPORTUNITIES

What the media keep calling the poorest country in the western hemisphere is, in fact, sitting on a gold mine. Haiti's natural resources, including actual gold, are estimated at $20 billion. Following the earthquake, American and Canadian firms started doing exploration.[37]

The African continent has a massive amount of natural resources, like diamonds, sugar, salt, gold, iron, cobalt, uranium, and more.[38] The youngest populations in the world are

---

37 (Norris McDonald 2019)
38 (EFFICA-GROUP n.d.)

found on the African continent.[39] Haiti has more than half of the population under the age of twenty-five with an unemployment rate of 40 percent; this is to say the most valuable resource of the BOP is people, and for the most part, young people.[40]

People often think that the poorest countries don't have natural resources, but just from these few statements, we can agree that's a false assumption. Bottom of the pyramid communities aren't lacking natural resources. The issue is how to leverage the resources for the good of the majority. Many experts found a correlation of greater inequality in places where resources are explored to just the benefit of the few, something they call the "resource curse."[41]

There's massive wealth to explore at the bottom of the pyramid. All the problems cited earlier come with an opportunity to create new market innovations in certain sectors. The opportunities to create new products and services are unlimited and can result in massive growth.

INSIDE THE MIND OF THE POOR

At the BOP, we are in survival mode. Every day is a new day to start a new battle for a better life; the fight is constant and brutal, and we're fragile. Some of us have given up and let the universe take its course, but many continue to wake up, try new things, solve problems, and work for whatever outcome they can produce.

---

39 (IGHOBOR 2013)
40 (Central Intelligence Agency n.d.)
41 (Tran 2012)

In 2016, at the University of California, Berkeley I met with former President Bill Clinton during the Clinton Global Initiative. While we were speaking, I told him, "Mr. President, I understand all the work you are trying to in the world and in Haiti, but you need to involve the people in more. Because something worse than poverty is the belief you will always be poor. When you have this belief, you know you are condemned to a life of poverty—when you cross this line, there's little that can be done to save that person. His or her behavior will be proportional to his or her belief in possibility. In hope. Accomplishing what the psychologists might call a self-fulfilling prophecy. Our beliefs reinforce our expectations, our expectations reinforce our behavior and produce the results we get. The cycle continues, making us more vulnerable and steals our humanity little by little."

A mindset revolution is a need at the BOP and this can only be done by the underdogs who have accomplished the seemingly impossible. Reigniting the spirit of innovation and hope based on good policy changes and decisions is the first step in turning the pyramid upside down.

CONCLUSION

The bottom of the pyramid is complex to understand and it's not homogeneous. The few elements presented in this chapter are based on my limited worldview and experience living in Haiti. Many of these need to be addressed and discussed with people in BOP communities and you are also free to add other elements that might give us a more accurate picture of what the BOP looks like as shown in the famous book *Fortune at the Bottom of the Pyramid*. Even though we use the concept

"BOP" to talk about underserved communities, we need to be clear that this label cannot in any way encompass all communities and is not an excuse not to try to understand and study each community specifically.

If the base of the pyramid stays frail, sooner or later it will crumble. On an individual or institutional level, consider collecting data before taking any course of action and, more importantly, dive into the stories of those you seek to serve, not just to empathize but to understand. I believe the same way Muhammad Ali beat Joe Frazier in the fourteenth round on October 1, 1975, in Manila, the success of the BOP will surprise the world. And this data should inspire us to see the opportunities to foster growth and unleash innovation at the bottom of the pyramid.

CHAPTER THREE

LIMITATIONS OF THE TOP-DOWN INNOVATION APPROACH

Innovation is the central issue in economic prosperity.
— MICHAEL PORTER

There's this famous story in the international development sector about an organization that wanted to save a disadvantaged community by providing water. This non-profit organization goes to a poor community with drinking water issues to solve their problems. In this village, the inhabitants usually walk two to three hours to get to the closest natural water source to carry back a bucket of five gallons that cannot last more than a day.

Witnessing the pain of the people walking such long distances to get five gallons of water, this organization wanted to come up with a solution. They assessed the geological characteristics of the soil in the area and found a water table. So, they dug a well and installed a water pump that was only a fifteen-minute walk from the village. After accomplishing the good deeds, they invited the villagers to inaugurate and celebrate this important realization.

Two weeks later, they noticed people weren't going to the brand new well they installed. The villagers were still walking two to three hours to get one small bucket of water. Puzzled, the initiators of the project gathered a group of villagers to find out what happened. Right in the middle of the conversation, they realized why the villagers were no longer going to the well.

This had nothing to do with water and the villagers were not dumb. They came to find out that going to the natural source was a moment for the villagers to spend time with each other, gossip about what's happening in the village, and meet boyfriends and girlfriends. In their basic need for water was hidden a strong need for socialization.

What if they had asked these questions before coming up with a solution?

What could happen if they had involved the villagers in the design process? If they knew this truth, how could they have provided better solutions?

THE TOP-DOWN INNOVATION

One of the most challenging factors of the top-down approach is only the ones at the top of the pyramid drive innovation and decide for the entire population. It's not out of hate or any malicious intent but because we've been conditioned by a top-down worldview. We view the world through the lens of grades, classes, and social groups. A top-down approach means a pre-selection has been made and others who could contribute are ignored or discarded based on social yardsticks that are not always logical.

Today, the market is more consumer-driven. Consumers are asking for their power and punishing big companies by withholding their hard-earned dollars. Communities are becoming louder and demanding that their voices be heard when it comes to solving social issues. From climate change to hunger and social rights, the community is asking to be heard. Understanding consumers and the community have become an essential part of the innovation process. Technology has to give a voice to the ones we used to ignore.

In the business world, research and development departments are asked to innovate. They would hire the "best" and "most creative" people who would work in secret for months in a lab to develop new products and services for the entire organization or market, often without involving other departments or the market they seek to serve. The management team comes with the company's mission statement and fabricates a culture in their lab to force upon employees. The top-down approach is based on this single belief: a group of apparent winners has the best answers to save the apparent helpless, and their skills are enough to solve the challenge of the majority.

In politics, business, and religions, a few have been anointed or have the power to decide on the fate of the majority.[42]

---

42 (Prabhu 2012)

How can seven billion people's fate be in the hands of 500 mortals who are all born with the same vices and potential for wisdom as the seven million? How has this worldview persevered through time?

There are two ways to enable innovation. The first way is to make a strong player stronger.[43] The second method is to empower the weak players. By empowering the first group, we confirm their intelligence. By empowering the second group, we tap into the unknown, the potential not yet explored. A person's origin does not impede their innovation or ability to come up with amazing ideas. Innovation and creativity know no gender, color, or class.

There's a certainty that those who are already strong players can win and create. There's nothing to surprise us here. If you have the resources, money, knowledge, or went to the Ivy League schools, we expect you to perform at the highest level; it's a fact, and we'll judge you if you don't. On the other hand, engaging the weak players, the ones who cannot make it, is a risk. Their chance to fail is as high as their chance to succeed. But their accomplishment is surprising and can have a high return on the community as well as inspire more people at the bottom to innovate.

The ones at the top might think they are saving the ones at the bottom, but the ones at the bottom don't see it that way. The middle class in the United States is fighting against the top 10 percent. The women are tired of men taking over everything and discriminating against them. The masses

---

43 (Gladwell 2017)

in Haiti are fighting against the intellectual and economic elite. From Hong Kong to France to Ecuador, the Underdog Revolution is happening. The mistrust between the top and the bottom of the pyramid is growing; this will continue to grow because of the wealth gap, health gap, collaboration gap, and blatant indifference. We would be foolish to think we can build a better world by defining the powerful as the enemy, and it would be dangerous to build a better world with a top-down approach or by not taking into consideration the ones we see as weak.

INTERNATIONAL AID THAT HURTS

Did you know that out of every dollar spent during the earthquake in Haiti, only one cent went to the government to help aid the people?[44] Let's consider international aid on a governmental and personal level.

On a governmental level, many rich countries help poor countries by providing financial and material resources, which is a really good thing, you might be saying. But let's take a deeper look. When it comes to financial resources, the countries that are helping come with their experts on poverty. These experts earn a big chunk of money, stay at the best hotels, eat the best food, and ironically try to figure out poverty's solution from books. When it comes to in-kind donations, they are often finite resources and not sustainable. Few aid agencies help the population become independent. Doing it would mean the end of their existence.

---

44 (CBS 2010)

On an individual level, people are most comfortable giving food, clothes, or other finite resources. I feel that a lot of people who give this kind of donation do it to feed their charity-persona. In other words, they feel obligated to do it and it makes them feel good about themselves, but their objective in giving is not to help these people get unstuck from the poverty cycle. It's easier to get people to donate food items and clothes instead of contributing to entrepreneurship ideas of people in developing countries. Why? I think it's difficult to grasp the idea of poor people turning into entrepreneurs and becoming independent. I hope I am wrong and that's not a reason.

I have difficulty understanding the idea of two or three nice people going to a poor country to donate pencils, notebooks, and candies to kids. I would better appreciate them as tourists. It's like giving Ibuprofen to cure a patient who has cancer. I think underserved communities are experiments for a lot of people. They go there to experience what is like to be poor, to see how blessed they are, and to do something to feel good about themselves. In summary, it's more about them than the ones in need.

If you want to help, come and help, but please do it with the idea of getting people unstuck. Come help build a school, a good one. Create a library with good books. Teach people how to code, create software, do voice-overs, speak and write your language. Help them start a business. We know you might want to teach them the Bible, but for God's grace, this cannot be the main thing you do. Don't save them. Show them the way to salvation and let them go on an adventure of discovery.

THE SAVIOR COMPLEX

"The bottom of the pyramid (BOP) is incapable of helping themselves."

"They need government assistance and international aid to help them."

"They cannot come up with solutions."

"They are uneducated and poor, they require a savior."

"A (insert prestigious education institution) graduate is revolutionizing sanitation in Africa."

How many times have you read similar lines in the media? Do you want to convince others that among the 10 million people living in a specific country, the only people who could solve the issues those 10 million people live within is someone coming from another place who doesn't understand the community? Or even speak the language? What's the difference between those smart people and those poor and living in the slums? Is it IQ? Is it creativity? Is it resources? Is it access?

Intelligence, creativity, and high IQ are not reserved for a class, a group, or a specific nation. It all comes down to three elements which I call the "Underdog Bermuda Triangle," which I explain in detail in Chapter 10.

To get back on topic, the same way an elite school grad or rich philanthropist can solve the issues in poor countries, many people in these communities could also solve these problems but are restricted from doing so. First, their community won't give them the chance to show what they can come up with. Second, organizations coming to these underserved communities won't spend time finding them or funding their ideas. In the end, people in the community and the foreigners assume that everybody in the underserved community needs a savior.

When underdogs don't get the chance to test their hypothesis and solutions for several years, they became sterile and start believing they are incapable. This cycle destroys the vulnerable communities by crushing the potential of other underdogs who could have changed things for the better. As the years pass, these communities become crippled by challenges, inequalities, and mediocrity. If this cycle continues, it's unlikely that these communities could ever come out of their dark years.

We need to rephrase "giving back to the community" to "going back to create with the community." When someone succeeds, the immediate goal should not be to just go back and dump blessings in the community but to utilize your blessings to help the community create their own blessings. The BOP doesn't need a savior: it needs a "potential explorer" and "human potential activator."

THE CREATOR IS AT THE CENTER
In the top-down approach to innovation, the creator is the most important element in the innovation process. His or her understanding of the issues is the lens through which she or he is solving the issues. The innovator relies solely on human experience and knowledge. The creator is implicated

throughout all the design processes and is often fragile about protecting her or his idea, which makes the process biased.

When the designer is the center of the design, it's becoming more about making the project or idea come to life. More often than not, market research becomes more about collecting data than understanding the humans they seek to serve. People are often seen as data providers instead of potential co-creators.

I would not argue that elite designers and innovators do not think about the market or community they seek to serve. However, when a project is centered around one individual's taste, protecting the ego can stand in the way of seeing.

UNINTENDED CONSEQUENCES OF GOOD ACTIONS
Good actions can also have bad consequences. All over the world, leaders, humanitarian organizations, and international aid agencies are flocking to the most vulnerable communities. Business magnates are working hard to come up with profitable solutions for the base of the pyramid—a 4.5 billion customer base with an economic value estimated at $5 trillion according to the World Bank.[45] While interest in helping the most vulnerable is growing over the years, failures to understand or improve the BOP have not decreased.

After the 2010 earthquake in Haiti that killed 200,000 people, the Bill and Melinda Gates Foundation created a $10 million fund to bring the mobile wallet to the BOP, because experts

---
45 (World Bank n.d.)

have seen its success in Africa and thought it would be as successful in Haiti. Nine years later, after more millions spent, the market penetration of mobile banking is still very low. In 2015, Haiti had 68.25 mobile cellular subscriptions per 100 inhabitants,[46] yet only 60,000 people having a mobile wallet in 2015 were active users,[47] and even today the user base is still very low. Is it because people don't want it? Did the foundation understand the real needs of the BOP when it comes to financial services?

"Developing New Market Opportunities for the Base of the Pyramid" is a program launched in Mexico in 2006 by the Inter-American Development Bank's Multilateral Investment Fund and the Mexican Business Council's Private Sector Study Commission for Sustainable Development, which aim to encourage big Mexican companies to develop inclusive business ventures. In an article published in 2013 on Devex.com, Ezequiel Reficco, professor of strategy at the Universidad de Los Andes School of Management in Colombia, said the following about the program:

"It had all the makings of success: a large population of underserved consumers, a growing economy, and local companies with the research and development capacity to make innovation happen. After 186 awareness sessions, sixty-five general workshops, and thirteen focused workshops—and in spite of generous offers of financial support to participating companies—not a single project came to life."[48]

---

46   (Statista 19)

47   (González 2015)

48   (Reficco 2016)

We could cite many examples of large corporations and big non-profits failing at the BOP. Even when some succeeded with their bottom line or accomplished the project they set out to develop, it often comes at a high cost for the people living at the bottom of the pyramid. There are so many unintended consequences of doing good that they do not consider due to a lack of understanding by taking a top-down approach of the underlying culture of the community they seek to serve. Good intentions and good actions aren't enough to empower people at the bottom; cognitive empathy is.

CONCLUSION

Justice means getting everybody a fair shot in every aspect of life. I am not advocating to destroy the elites, because even when you empower the BOP, an elite group will always emerge as a natural part of life. What I am advocating for is for the top to open the innovation floor for people at the base of the pyramid to also come and play with their ideas.

The top-down approach has atrophied the potential of the bottom of the pyramid and makes it infertile. Now it's time to stimulate a new stream of ideas, innovation, and movement by and for the BOP. Our likelihood of building a better world for the most vulnerable increases when we invert the pyramid of innovation. When we engage them as problem solvers in the potential solutions. We can organize real think tanks, live where they live, feel their pain, and include them in the innovation process.

Let us begin a new era, an era not based on saving the seemingly helpless but empowering them to help themselves.

Genius ideas are dying right now in the slums of Brazil, innovations that the world would never see that are locked in jails in the United States, world-changing movements that are slowly disintegrating in underserved communities. But they will never see the light of day if the innovation only comes from the top.

CHAPTER FOUR

THE LINK BETWEEN CONSTRAINTS AND CREATIVITY

I think frugality drives innovation, just like other constraints do. One of the only ways to get out of a tight box is to invent your way out.

— JEFF BEZOS

We were running out of money, and we could not continue repairing the space we rented. I thought everything was under control; my co-founder David would be able to raise enough money in the United States. I would simply execute the vision we worked on at the WeWork office of 222 South Riverside Plaza in Chicago. The space was in terrible condition. It did not have lights, switches, doors, windows, even the floor was broken and ugly. It was a mess. The first time I saw it, I said, "Shit, we've made a mistake."

In 2014, I attended the Clinton Global Initiative University Conference, a Clinton Foundation's program for change-makers around the world in Phoenix, Arizona.' The event gathers experts, change agents, mentorship networks, and financial resources for three days for an engaging and inspiring conference. It aims to support students from all over the world who are looking to address the world's most pressing challenges in a creative way.

During that conference, I ended up as a finalist for the Resolution Project (a CGIU partner social venture competition) and met some impactful leaders; and one of them would pave my way to the work I am currently doing. While pitching my venture idea, the Haitian flag attracted a young black woman named Moreen Tony to my colorful booth. As we started chatting, we found out we used to live in the same neighborhood in Haiti when we were younger. We kept in touch after the conference and our relationship grew over the years.

One evening while browsing Facebook at my cousin's dance studio in Pétion-Ville, I received a phone notification from a Facebook group named "Haitian In San Francisco." I clicked on it and saw that Moreen had tagged me under a post of David Pierre-Louis's, stating "a Haitian living in Seattle visiting San Francisco who wanted to open a coworking space in Haiti." Her comment went like this: *"If you are going to work around entrepreneurship in Haiti, you need to meet Pierre."* After I liked the comment, I befriended David on Facebook. Forty-five minutes later, David had Skyped me and we decided to work together on an event called '"FuckUp Nights" that never happened because Category Five hurricane Matthew hit and affected a million Haitians on October 4, 2016.

While we could not do the event, we decided to raise money to provide food and water filtration systems to more than thirty families in Port-au-Prince and Kenscoff. Following the urgent needs of food that we satisfied, I raised around $5,000 to provide seeds and goats for more than 200 farmers in my mother's hometown. Based on their testimony, some have generated more than $200 in sales after harvest. We recently visited and were happy to also see a home for a man whose house the hurricane destroyed. Today when my mom visits my grandma, the villagers are always manifesting their gratitude. We helped them with shared dignity—they did not have to fight for it, and we walked more than four hours in a dark night to go to them.

After this experience, David invited me to join his team in planning and launching **Impact Hub Port-au-Prince**, a co-working space and entrepreneurial community focused on social impact and part of the larger network of Impact Hub worldwide. It was already a year since I'd resigned from my managing position at an insurance company. I was also at the end of testing the entrepreneurship education program for high school students for which I was the finalist at the CGIU, so it was the right moment to start a new venture.

With teammates living and traveling in different parts of the world, the magnitude of the project hindered us and everything stalled for at least a year. Fast forward to 2017, a storm wrecked my life into pieces. The two businesses I started from my savings failed, adding to that a terrible breakup, then I spiraled into a depression where I would spend a whole day without food. With tears in my eyes, massive failures under my name, betrayal in my hands, but a spark of faith in my heart, I purchased a one-way ticket to go to Wausau, Wisconsin and never come back to Haiti.

My days in Wausau were for the most part good because of my former host mother Joanne Lapinski. Some days I could not get out of bed, but other days I would write and work on my goals. During my time in Wausau, David and I stayed in touch. One day after almost an hour on the phone, we decided to meet in Chicago. David flew from Seattle and a friend of mine dropped me at a Starbucks in Chicago. We spent a day and a half strategizing in a colorful meeting room at WeWork. We worked on a budget, planning, and space repair (a space one of the other co-founders rented while I was away), and go-to-market strategy. After our long day meeting, I flew back to Port-au-Prince to launch the first local hub and co-working space in Haiti with a global imprint.

A few months later, I realized the funds we expected would not come and we would need to shift strategy. Frustrated and feeling cornered, I did not want to wait for more resources. I could not hire professional workers, so I gathered a group of volunteers to help us clean, paint, and do other repair work in exchange for membership when we opened. Things that were supposed to cost hundreds of dollars ended up costing almost 40 percent less. With two of my former employees, Myrlene Mathurin and Berline Pierre, who were underdogs with extraordinary talents, we worked every day at the space. With no running water, we would buy gallons of drinking water to shower after our back-hurting intensive days of manual labor.

We couldn't afford an expensive working table, so we designed our table and hired a woodworker to execute it. When you design what you want, it costs less (but ignorance has a price). We couldn't afford to replace the broken and old flooring, so we found a YouTube video that taught us to use a specific kind of technique to repaint the ceramic floor. We could not afford a good optical fiber, so I upgraded my home router and carried it every morning to the hub and left with it at night. After months of working tirelessly, the space started to look better. Even though we were not ready to open officially, I decided to pre-sell two of our most expensive memberships and use that money to prepare the office space for our first clients, who were two young entrepreneurs. All of this with only two inverter batteries, a 500-watt inverter, and a small 1,000-watt generator. In the midst of all of the struggles, we organized a Startup Week for more than 400 entrepreneurs, where we turned competitors and other actors in the entrepreneurial ecosystem into partners to organize events in their space and get access to resources that they had, a model that has been since copied by other local organizations. You can't compete with your weak points; you have to turn competitors into partners for the good of the people you serve. The ego has almost no place.

For an entire year, I could not afford a dime. At some point, I had to move to a friend's house. There were days where I had to choose between eating well and taking care of the Hub. As we grew, we bought new batteries, a brand-new automatic inverter, and a 5,000-watt generator that broke seven months later, so we had to rent one almost daily from a partner organization to keep our company alive. When we started officially, we could not attract members at the BOP as we set out to do, so we came up with a daily membership called "Jounen Fokis" that enabled our potential members to pay an equivalent of $2.70 per day to access our space instead of the monthly membership. To engage our diaspora, we also create a membership that we are still refining that also enables local entrepreneurs to access our resources. With only eight hours of electricity at night, when space is closed, we saw an opportunity to create a new event named #HustleNights where people would come to our space to work on a specific goal for two nights, which was always a success. Serving people with lower purchase power is a financial struggle, but seeing them thrive and grow is a human and emotional reward. Seeing our entrepreneurs pitch, build their websites, open bank accounts, and get their own space is the beginning of the impact we set out to make.

We are still not financially profitable, but now I can pay myself and two other people. We now have Henry Miller Chairs, a Conference room for fifteen people, event space and shared workspace, dedicated desks, better internet, more members, and three different programs for entrepreneurs: *Academy Of Women Entrepreneurship*, which we run with the United States Embassy in Haiti; *ZEL*, which provides a workspace and thirty-four weeks training to seventeen entrepreneurs; and we recently hosted the fourth edition of *Startup Week*, the largest and most inclusive entrepreneurial event in Port-au-Prince, welcoming more than 1,200 attendees, sixty-five speakers, and fifty volunteers. While writing this, I just secured $20,000 in funding to start a co-creating space where creators at the BOP will have access to tools, machinery, and resources to allow them to create and innovate. Our space has become a community where coders, leaders, creators, and designers meet, network, and create amazing ventures with social impact. We are still facing constraints: there are still things that don't work *yet*, but we never let the constraints define us. Our constraints were supposed to wreck us and break our minds but instead created a stronger us. As Ryan Holiday says in his book *The Obstacle Is the Way*:

"Certain things in life will cut you open like a knife. When that happens—at that exposing moment—the world gets a glimpse of what's truly inside you. So what will be revealed when you're sliced open by tension and pressure? Iron? Or air? Or bullshit?"

When constraints cut us open, it found creativity.

LET'S DEFINE CREATIVITY

The word "creativity" came from the Latin term "*creare*" meaning "to create, to make." But its current meaning only emerged during the Age of Reason, the eighteenth century termed "the Century of Philosophy."

According to the Oxford Dictionary, creativity is the use of **imagination** or original ideas to create something. Based on this definition, we can all agree that every human being with a functional brain is capable of imagining. Other than the academic definition of creativity, throughout the years many people have given a personal meaning to this word based on their own experience with the creative process.

Chief Operating Officer Sonia Simone of Rainmaker Digital defines creativity as "just making something. It might be something crummy or awkward or not ready for prime time. If you make something, you are creative." While Simone's creativity is about simply making something, well-known blogger and *Brain Pickings* founder Maria Popova has a more complex way of defining creativity. She sees creativity as the ability to connect the seemingly unconnected and meld existing knowledge into new insights about some elements of how the world works. That's practical creativity. Then there's moral creativity: to apply that skill toward some kind of wisdom on how the world *ought* to work.[49] For the sake of understanding in this book, we will define creativity as the **ability to create something (emotional, physical) that stretches your imagination while utilizing resources available at your disposal.**

When looking at all the definitions above, we can all agree that there's no mention of group, class, gender, or nationality. Therefore, if creativity is an act of creating something or the use of imagination, it's fair to say, to some degree, *every* human (including people at the BOP) is capable of being creative or can participate in the creative process. Whether some people are born with more ability to create or learn to be creative is not the question. The fact is we are all capable of bringing to the world objects, ideas, and movements with our own unique touch.

The wall in front of us is not always an obstacle; it can also be a space for a door or a window. While the current worldview believes that constraints stifle creativity, countless studies prove that constraints or scarcity are some of the key elements that lead to creativity, hence the term creative-constraints.

---

49 (Stillman 2016)

CONSTRAINTS BREED CREATIVITY

After analyzing more than 162 innovation processes using the questions, "How should an enterprise go about inventing something novel and useful? Is there a structured thinking process that reliably produces results?" the *World Database of Innovation*'s researchers discovered that while each creative process varies from another, they all have a common denominator: 'scarcity". They also found that deliberate creative constraints push us to see what our eyes could not see and stretch our imagination where it could not go before. Solutions that came from creative constraints get greater success in the marketplace than the ones generated from simple blue-skies mode (curiosity).[50]

Every individual faces a set of constraints on a daily basis and has to navigate them in order to survive. While these constraints might come from our mere existence as human beings, they shift our worldview, force us to change our habits, and improve the way we live. In the creative process, constraint plays a role of catalyst, it tells us something is not working, it tests our assumptions, and it asks to find a different way than the ones we had in mind before encountering the constraints.

The lives of people living at the bottom of the pyramid are filled with constraints, from food to sanitation to education to finances. The one thing that's not scarce to the BOP is constraint. Considering that people living in the BOP want a better life for their families and themselves, they are constantly trying, thinking, and forcing themselves to come up with a way to survive. Creative constraints become a natural

---

50 (Neren 2011)

part of their daily lives. Not facing these constraints can result in staying hungry for days, getting kicked out of school, losing a job, and even losing their lives. The cost of the constraints in the BOP is too high not to address them. While the majority of the people have to face these constraints just to survive, without a doubt we can assume that if given a little more adequate resources, they would be able to come with more long-term and sustainable creative solutions to their daily life challenges, because the constraints push them to be more creative.

When operating in an environment with an abundance of resources, people tend to choose the first available option that comes to them, which results in surface-level thinking. In an environment where resources are scarce, we are forced to think deeper and go beyond surface-level thinking to come up with solutions that are innovative and not apparent. In a 2015 study that examined how scarcity or abundance influences creativity, Ravi Mehta at the University of Illinois and Meng Zhu at Johns Hopkins University found as we become a more abundant society, our aggregate average creativity levels decrease. Mehta also supported my argument that people at the BOP have more ability to create when she said, *"If you look at people who don't have resources or only have limited resources, they actually end up being more creative with what they have. If you go to a poor country and see how they solve problems by repurposing older products, it's super innovative."* When times are tough, resource-poor people become more creative in their use of everyday products.[51] Based on this new shared evidence, I think it's time that the

---

51 (CICIORA 2015)

world aid agencies, international corporations, and charity organizations interested in making an impact in the BOP involve the poor in the creative process.

According to an article published on February 7, 2017, by Scott Sonenshein, a professor at the Jesse H. Jones School of Business, Rice University and author of the book *Stretch*, he stated the following:

"*Our environments, in other words, either impel us to see things differently or they don't. That implies that creativity is in many ways situational, not some inborn faculty or personality trait. When people face scarcity, they give themselves the freedom to use resources in less conventional ways—because they have to. The situation demands a mental license that would otherwise remain untapped.*"[52]

Martin Luther King's dream did not become a reality *in spite* of racism, it became a reality *because* of racism.

The Wright brothers did not invent the airplane in spite of not having resources that Samuel Langley had, they invented the plane because they *did not have* the resources Langley had.

The Haitian revolution did not happen in spite of slavery, it happened *because* of slavery.

Underdogs build their strength on the curveballs the current social measurement system throws at them.

---

52 (SONENSHEIN 2017)

THE TOOLBOX FALLACY

Samuel Langley was educated, backed by the establishment, and had all the money he needed to invent the first airplane, but history will always remember the Wright brothers as the inventors of the first airplane even when there are NSA spaces named after Langley.[53]

How can we explain an individual with a filled toolbox who produces less than one with fewer tools?

After years of observation and personal experience, I have come to this conclusion: "The quantity and quality of the tools are not the decisive factors. The *way* the tools are used are. It's not about the tools, it's about how you use your tools." This is what we commonly call resourcefulness. Blessings are not always good things, sometimes they are a curse, and more often than not, curses can also be disguised as blessings.

Research and development spending overall increased 11.4 percent in 2018, to a record high of $782 billion according to a report of the 2018 *Global Innovation 1000* study, and companies selected as the most innovative outperformed the biggest research and developing spenders on a range of financial metrics. The study found little correlation between the vast amount of resources spent and innovation. How can the firms that hire the best people and spend the most money not be the most innovative? Simple: more resources don't necessarily lead to more innovation.[54]

---

53 (Lienhard n.d.)
54 (Barry Jaruzelski 2018)

Innovation departments in companies believe the more resources, more money (input) they use, the more innovative output they will generate. This is what I call the toolbox fallacy. This is the tendency to keep accumulating tools because of the belief that a better toolbox is what makes innovative creators. It's so ingrained in us that when interviewing successful creators, we always want to know the type of pens, notebooks, and paint they use. We think if we have the same tools, we will be able to create the same type of work. We ignore hard work, deliberate practice, and the power of constraints in favor of the fancy.

CONCLUSION

The lack of tools in the BOP is not an impediment to creativity. Innovators and creators at the BOP rise from the trash, the junkyard, to create a windmill as I tell the story of William Kamkwamba in Chapter 9.

There are too many people at the BOP practicing creative survival, where their creativity only allows them to survive. Because of the intense daily stress, they are constantly on the edge trying to solve an urgent problem linking to their very existence. We need to move from surviving to thriving. It's the right moment for the International Aid Agencies working on the SDGs to brainstorm solutions with local creators and innovators in the BOP in order to transform the creative-survival approach to a more flourishing creative approach.

Yes, the poor and people in underserved communities are creative. All we need to do is channel their creative ideas and visions into solutions. To do so, we need to create a playground where they can practice and enhance their creative skills. The same way jails exist to punish bad behavior, we need to design spaces to encourage those at the bottom of the pyramid to create and train their creative muscles.

Local governments in underserved communities should prioritize helping its citizens move from creative survival to creative problem solving by designing programs and training that removes unnecessary stress in their minds to unlock a flow of creativity that could contribute to decreased importation and reduce the number of undocumented people in the rich countries. Because what's more important for any human than the feeling of being useful and the sensation of progress? If people can use their creativity for their collective well-being, their view of themselves will change. They will no longer be victims but change agents. It will no longer be a few of us thriving; it will be most of us leveraging our constraints to creatively solve our common problems. To quote Malcolm Gladwell:

"*There is a set of advantages that have to do with material resources, and there is a set that has to do with the absence of material resources—and the reason underdogs win as often as they do is that the latter is sometimes every bit the equal of the former.*"

PART TWO

TURNING THE PYRAMID UPSIDE DOWN

CHAPTER FIVE

LEVELING THE PLAYING FIELD

―――

During my lifetime, I have dedicated myself to the struggle of the African people. I have fought against white domination, and I have fought against black domination. I have cherished the ideal of a democratic and free society in which all persons live together in harmony and with equal opportunities. It is an ideal which I hope to live for and to achieve. But if needs be, it is an ideal for which I am prepared to die.

— NELSON MANDELA

If all I am exposed to is violence, don't expect me to become a neurosurgeon. The output generated in BOP countries are in direct proportionality to their input. Yes a few of us, like the following story, would certainly surmount the challenges and overcome the systemic and social barriers. But it will be hundreds of years until you can expect the least developed countries (LCDs) to create large scale innovation unless we level the playing field.⁵⁵ You wouldn't ask your pastor who only studied theology to build your power grid system. So how can we expect exponential advancement from LCD's playing on an uneven playing field?

More than 400,000 residents live in extreme poverty in Cité Soleil (City of Sun), which is located in the Port-au-Prince metropolitan area in Haiti. Regarded as the poorest and most dangerous neighborhood in the Western Hemisphere, Cité Soleil is often controlled by groups of gangs leading different areas of the neighborhood. This is a place that used to evoke trembling fear; most people living in Port-au-Prince, including myself, would avoid it at all costs until recently. Now, floods of business people, college students, diaspora members, and leaders are posting pictures on social media of their visit to Cité Soleil. What changed? What happened to the poorest and most dangerous neighborhood in the Western Hemisphere?

In 2015, a group of young people in Cité Soleil said they wanted to build a library. They sat down and decided not to ask the government or any international aid agencies for financial support; they wanted it to be built by the community. Their vision was to create something massively transformational to inspire Haiti for generations to come. As one of the co-founders of this community-led project mentioned, *"We want Haiti's change to start with Cité Soleil."*

Their revolution is happening. They continually engage with their supporters, and they are often seen in pictures with

---

55   ('Utoikamanu n.d.)

almost everyone who donated to the project. Fast forward to 2019: The first floor is built and part of it is already open for students to come read and for the community to host meetings and events.

Cité Soleil is building the largest library not just in Haiti but in the Caribbean. Konbit Blibliyotèk Site Solèy has now become a model that other neighborhoods in Haiti are using to create their community center. Led by Louino Robillard and other young people in the community, the project mobilizes people all over Haiti to donate bricks, money, and books to build the largest library in the Caribbean Basin.

Instead of organizing birthday parties, people would turn their birthday into brick parties where they would give bricks to build the library. The movement has now left the frontier of Haiti as more Haitians and people living abroad are joining to create a legacy that will change how people view Cité Soleil and how Cité Soleil views itself.

People in Cité Soleil own the project and feel proud to be at the forefront of major milestones in Haiti's history. From an underdog community, a place filled with gangsters, the library is becoming the largest community-driven project in the country. How is that possible? How can we help other vulnerable communities to do the same? How do we level the playing field for other communities at the BOP?

Obvious winners and underdogs are playing on the same field but each on a different level. The playing field is uneven; opportunities, environment, resources, and support are all unbalanced. While we agree that everybody is born with some advantages—intellectual, social, financial or emotional—it's society's job to create an environment that's favorable to the winners, but that is also favorable to the ones with fewer resources. I think it's logical that the field is more neutral and not skewed for one category of people, but in today's world, the field is skewed for the high IQ, beautiful body, and people who meet the other social metrics we humans have created.

It's time to stop measuring people based on social yardsticks. Removing these measurements is about making sure that the world standard modeled around the typical apparent winner is not a model on which we want to build this future we are looking forward to. There are millions of people with the potential to create change but who are hindered by many factors. Without removing these barriers, the Underdog Revolution would not be possible. Based on my observation and research, I am presenting a few factors (you can add more) that I think should be regulated in order to level the playing field.

ACCESS TO FOOD

Every Monday during my break-time at my corporate job, my motorcycle guy and I would ride fifteen miles from the warm Port-au-Prince to the mountain-curvy road and thirty-degree Celsius weather in Kenscoff. In 2016, I started an entrepreneurial mindset development program for high school students in Kenscoff, located in the West Department of Haiti. The program provides financial literacy and entrepreneurship education to disadvantaged high school students living on less than a dollar a day. For one hour, we would introduce the students to creative thinking, scarcity mindset, problem-solving, personal finance and marketing, and through classroom-style engaging settings and product creation came together to create a product. This program was aimed at one overarching goal: changing the students' mindset from "*I am destined to be poor*" to "*I can create something useful with what's around me.*"

A few weeks into the program, we started having low attendance. For a class of forty-five students, only fifteen people would show up. At first, we thought the students did not like the program and did not find it useful, but when started asking questions, we discovered the untold story: students who come to school on empty stomachs cannot learn past 2 p.m. We did not have a budget to provide food, but we started giving crackers and juice at our sessions and we saw a big increase in our attendance and more engagement. Additionally, students also face a dilemma with little pocket money (the equivalent of 15 cents) because they have to choose between buying something to eat, paying taxis, or buying school supplies. We also tackled the second part of the problem by creating a local campaign to collect school supplies which we distribute every year to more than 500 students in Kenscoff. Mixing these two actions together drastically changed the value of our program and our students' ability to engage with the content. When eating is a struggle, it's almost impossible to convince someone to think creatively.

The United Nations Food and Agriculture Organization (FAO) estimates that about 815 million people of the 7.6 billion people in the world, or 10.7 percent, were suffering from chronic undernourishment in 2016. Almost all the hungry people live in lower-middle-income countries, but there are also 11 million people undernourished in *developed* countries.[56] Undernourishment leads to poor health performance and low brain function. A 2007 study conducted by Professor Aisa Mendoza-Salonga of the University of Philippines, Manilla, concluded: *"Nutrition plays a major role in the development of the nervous system. Studies have shown that malnutrition causes a variety of cognitive and behavioral deficits over a lifetime. The severity, timing, and duration of malnutrition are important determinants of its possible effect on the neurological development of the child."* Undernourishment and malnutrition decrease the intelligence of people living at the bottom of the pyramid.[57]

Local governments, world organizations, and other institutions should continue working actively to ensure local agriculture reflects the nutrients needed for brain development or leverage tech to develop food that can supercharge brain power and also solve hunger issues. By increasing access to food, we will automatically increase people's ability to think clearer and participate in the world we want for our children.

CREATE A SECURE ENVIRONMENT

When poverty is wrecking your life, a lack of safety makes seeking a better life even more difficult. In the past year, violence has drastically increased in Haiti due to political instability. Imagine constantly fearing for your life, not because you do anything wrong, but because you simply exist. On October 6, 2019, Marc Alain Boucicault, co-founder of a co-working space in Port-au-Prince, while on crutches, sat

---

56 (Food and Agriculture Organization of the United Nations 2019)

57 (Mendoza-Salonga 2104)

and watched on his live cam dozens of people breaking into his business. The space he poured his economy and soul into was being ransacked in broad daylight. Strangers stole all his furniture and goods as he watched.

Political instability, coups, and illegitimate governments are among the largest causes of insecurity in underserved communities. Government services are not present so, in the absence of legitimate leaders, by default bandits become the leaders. They control specific areas and turn other young people into gang members who cannot escape from their grip.

The same way gang leaders can encourage and force young people to continue their evil work, the opposite is also possible. We could also create sustainable alternatives where those trapped in violence can begin to recover their human dignity and desire for significance as human beings. An article published in the *British Medical Journal* on February 9, 2002, said: "*Eight out of ten of the world's poorest countries are suffering, or have recently suffered, from large-scale violent conflict. Wars in developing countries have heavy human, economic, and social costs and are a major cause of poverty and underdevelopment.*"[58]

Humans committing evil is probably a permanent part of the human condition, but creating an environment conducive to violence is also a crime.

Local governments and social establishments should stop buying and distributing guns to people in underserved communities. And if they fail at these tasks, it's incumbent to the

---

58 (F. Stewart 2002)

United Nations (UN) to reestablish peace in these affected communities and these governments whether or not they are supported by economically powerful countries. We all know underserved communities don't *produce* crack, cocaine, and other drugs. I was shocked when I visited North Lawndale, Chicago in 2013 to learn that more than 70 percent of all North Lawndale men between the ages of eighteen and forty-five have a criminal record, three times higher than the average statistics in the United States.[59] People in underserved communities are too poor to afford an AR-15. Those semi-automatic rifles are given to them by the legal bandits. The same way some religious groups exploit the poverty factor in underserved communities to grow their fellowship, legal bandits and gangs exploit the vulnerability of young people in the BOP. As we create avenues and growth opportunities, the less those young people will be vulnerable to work that destroys their own community and BOP'ers like themselves.

DUMP LESS

Haiti imports more than $3 billion worth of goods annually compared to $900 million exported, according to the CIA World Factbook.[60] When looking to help underserved communities, the surface level thinking approach is to dump resources to the ones in need without thinking about the unintended consequences of these resources. In good conscience, people and organizations want to help and they are doing it using the only model available to them. Every time you donate or send something to poor countries, ask yourself these questions:

---

59 (GLANTON 2017)

60 (Central Intelligence Agency n.d.)

- Who is going to be affected, and how will it affect the quality of life of the recipients?

- Is that something that can be easily found, bought, or produced locally?

- Are there any other elements needed to make sure they can make good use of it?

- Is there something equivalent I could do that would exponentially increase the lives of the people I seek to serve?

In high school, I did not own a computer. I learned graphic design by standing behind someone's desk. I worked for my clients at a friend's house and would even sleep at his house sometimes. Imagine how a functional computer would change my life compared to a few tennis shoes. Imagine how many of us want to do good but don't think about the unintended consequences.

The dumping from top to bottom takes multiple forms. For example, if a solution works in a country in Africa, experts would flock to Haiti to apply it, assuming that would also work. I have heard this statement several times, *"This is a solution that has worked across Africa."* Okay, but Haiti is not Africa. Every year, the world's richest countries dump a ton of electronic waste in poor countries.

The dumping of ideas, products, charity, and trash should be stopped in favor of collaboration, co-creation, and fair-trade deal.

If you can make it, buy it at a fair price, or create it in the BOP, do it there. Chose local.

If we, the BOP, are always *given* ideas, food, and other resources, it will be impossible for us to come up with innovative ideas on our own. We'll never become self-sufficient. If you want to design communication support for a community, do it with the local businesses in that community. The world needs to dump less and empower more.

INVOLVE THEM IN THE DECISION PROCESS
How many poor people are involved in Davos, the World Economic Forum, and other major platforms where they discuss the fate of the BOP? Big decisions about the destiny of communities in the BOP are made without their involvement. It's often in the news that we hear about the solutions and projects for our communities and countries. There are very few organizations that organize community listening sessions. I have been in a few of these meetings they are often more interested in convincing you to adopt their prefabricated ideas instead of being open to new ideas and collaboration.

Local community buy-in is more important than the local generation of ideas. So local people play the game because they don't want the project, opportunity, or support to go away even when they do not believe it will work. Even when they know projects have no long-term impact, lots of people at the BOP will accept to play the game to earn a few dollars to support their families and communities through jobs provided in the project. As they say in Haiti, "*Chen grangou pa jwe,*" the hungry dog doesn't play.

We can invite these people we seek to serve in the high-level meetings and events so they share their stories and also share their solutions and ideas. Fly economically challenged people from the countryside of Bangladesh or Congo to the UN meeting when we discuss their fate. Let them paint you a picture of the future they envision and you would be surprised to discover the wisdom you've been missing.

CREATE MORE LABS AND RESEARCH CENTERS THAN PRISONS

Do not fail in our name, let us fail for ourselves.

In the social development sector and in the business world, trial and error are at the core of great innovation. When it comes to the bottom of the pyramid, experts and businesses are failing in our name. International organizations are doing trial and error for us. The top of the pyramid is testing what's working for the base of the pyramid instead of providing them with space and resources to test hypotheses and ideas.

If through the trial and error process, money and resources are being used, who would be better suited to use it than the ones affected by the problem? This why I advocate for local governments, aid agencies, and charity organizations to start creating more labs instead of short-term projects that make them look good.

Underdog communities and individuals will thrive when we start building space for these communities to research, ideate, prototype, and test ideas. For instance, only seven scientific and technical journal articles were published in 2013 for every million people in Africa.⁶¹ Creating local labs would serve as a playground for these communities to develop breakthrough ideas that could solve challenging problems they are facing.

Instead of investing millions of dollars in product dumping and using the BOP as experimental space, I assume organizations would make a more long-term impact by creating:

- Medical labs
- Chemical labs
- Prototyping labs
- Computer labs
- Coding labs
- Agriculture and food transformation labs
- Waste management plants
- Research labs
- Woodworking labs

These labs' goals would not be to commercialize products; their aim is to allow these underdog communities to see their potential, widen their horizon, and come up with breakthrough ideas that government, non-profit, and investors can scale.

FINANCIAL INCLUSION

My friend Dez and I were working on a business venture named Boujonnen Botanic. The idea was to mix Haitian plants with fruits and other American tea leaves to access the US market. Our first roadblock was shipping; to ship the tea

---

61   ('Utoikamanu n.d.)

samples to Dez, I had to send them through a friend traveling in the States because of the high price. The shipping price was 30 percent more than the production cost.

Second, we discovered that Paypal, Venmo, and other financial payment platforms don't work with the Haitian Market. There's no legal way for us to use those services unless we have a US bank account or use someone who lives in the United States as a proxy. From these two examples, you can understand the difficulty that underdog entrepreneurs face when trying to access a global market. After all, 1.7 billion adults worldwide still lack a basic bank account according to the World Bank.[62]

To level the playing field, we need these unicorn companies like Alibaba, Paypal, and Amazon to open their platform to our world instead of dumbed-down technology alternative that takes away our dignity. While other countries are making a profit on our backs, they are closing their market to us. Of course, there are a few corporations in small countries that access the global market, but it's almost impossible for underdog ventures to grow their revenues by selling to people who cannot afford to pay for services and products they create. The same way ventures at the top can access the bottom market, it's fair to demand that small entrepreneurs at the bottom be allowed to access richer markets.

When people get access to financial products, they are more likely to use other services such as insurance, loans, and online marketplaces, which can exponentially change their

---

62 (World Bank 2017)

way of life. Banks won't loan to the poor without data. Imagine for a second if the million street sellers in Haiti could track their sales data connected to a central server monitored by the government and financial institutions. Imagine the massive change that could lead to.

TECHNOLOGY

The cost of a 3D printer has fallen from several thousand dollars to as low as $200.[63] From 2009 to 2017, the price for solar panels dropped 76 percent.[64] It's easier than ever to add such devices in the BOP. You are probably asking how do people who are fighting to eat and survive use 3D printers? Let me tell you a little story.

One Sunday morning, after an eighteen-minute run, I took a hot shower, went to the nail salon, and the supermarket. On my way back to the supermarket, I entered the public market. To put it in context, public markets are not the typical western farmers' market. It's often dirty, informal, and people are everywhere. After two minutes of walking, I found a *machann* (merchant in English) and purchased twenty-five cents worth of peppers (seven peppers). While getting my peppers I heard a few *machann* talking. When I turned my head, I saw five to six of them sitting on a bench. The conversation went like this:

The first one said, "Did you post it?"

---

63 (Nichols 2016)

64 (Bogmans 2019)

Another machann yelled, "You should post it!"

In my head, I was like, *What are they talking about?*

A third one replied, "No, she doesn't have Facebook."

Like a choir, they all responded, "Oooooh."

I was surprised to see people who cannot read yet own businesses that are worth around 400 dollars talking about Facebook in a way that makes them feel important. The same way Facebook penetrates that market, I would argue that other tech platforms that can change the vendors' lives and satisfy their needs for importance would work. Thus, it's up to the world, non-profits, profit-based businesses, and international agencies to introduce the underdog to the technology they can use to create new products and new services; and ultimately, to solve the problems of their community.

While low tech is being adopted by more people in the BOP, tech that can really make leapfrog changes are still foreign to underdogs and underdog communities. Most non-profits and international aid agencies fund projects that solve people's basic necessities. In part, it's very good to support the most pressing needs of the people, but it could be more impactful to also fund projects or ventures which introduce the base of the pyramid to technology that can improve their quality of life and widen their outlook.

I am excited about Elon Musk's ambitious SpaceX project called *Starlink*. They intend to launch a network of broadband satellites to provide high-speed internet on a global level, including in areas that did not previously have internet.[65] I can already foresee the changes and ideas, the businesses, that internet access will unleash in the BOP.

Soon people in richer countries or with more financial means will be able to control their home on a remote control. AI, blockchain, biotech, and robotics are changing lives in many countries already.[66] The Fourth Industrial Revolution is upon us. Will the BOP be able to get a part of it? This is a possible dream; I think we can do this. If we can go to the moon, we can improve the lives of the most vulnerable.

CONCLUSION
Leveling the playing field is a bedrock requirement for the Underdog Revolution I am foolishly preaching. If people at the BOP are playing the game in worse conditions, it's difficult for us to win. If the UN and the international aid agencies want us to grow and not be a burden for them, it's essential for the underdogs to be playing on the same playing field as the obvious winners. I did not mention corruption because it is a by-product of most of these factors.

The BOP is not a pot of gold for multinational exploitation. Nor is it a place for people who are living a good life to come to practice stoicism skills. It's a real place where real people exist and are looking for a better life. A life they want to earn in dignity and not through shame. I believe in a world where human beings are seen for who they can become. Not

---

65   (Etherington 2019)
66   ('Utoikamanu n.d.)

everyone in the world is a genius or a winner, but we need to create a world where everyone can *become* a success if they want to. Everyone deserves the tools and everyone deserves the opportunity.

Leveling the playing is not a favor that we are doing for the most vulnerable. Making the world a better place is our duty toward our children and the next generation. Closing the gap guarantees a more livable or lovable world where your sons and daughters would not be afraid to travel or be a victim of evil committed by people who could have been good citizens.

The playing field has been uneven for too long. It's time to even it up.

CHAPTER SIX

EMPOWERING THE DAVID'S OF THE WORLD

To strive to be the best version of yourself.

To constantly try to disrupt your past successes.

To be crazy enough to have unrealistic aspirations.

To be an underdog.

To be a stoic.

To be willing to walk straight through hell with a smile.

To unapologetically stand in your light when your demons are shouting your weaknesses.

To spread hope when self-doubt dabs in your mind.

To keep going with tears in your eyes, massive failures under your name, betrayal in your hand, but faith in your heart.

To experience the whole range of human emotions in a matter of seconds.

This is what it means to be a gladiator.

"President X sucks!"

"You suck!"

Here I was, screaming in the middle of a narrow street in Port-au-Prince, Haiti. Chanting and striking with a heated crowd, under a burning sun. Suddenly, I felt a tension in my body rising. My claws stuck out, and I slowly transformed into a violent activist who wanted to destroy everything in my way.

It wasn't supposed to turn out that way. I had a well thought out plan for my life. But here I was. Twenty-one, lost, no job, and no education. To make matters worse, an earthquake had hit Haiti, destroying almost everything and killing more than 200,000 people. The churches collapsed with my faith. I was pissed at God. My view of the future started to darken. During that short stint of radical activism, the unexpected happened. I got a scholarship for which I had been rejected the year before. I was lucky because it was not based on school performance but leadership involvement.

I arrived in the United States with a shitload of fears, preconceived notions, and biases. I'd been taught that America is racist, arrogant, and greedy. Like most of us, I grew up resenting other countries and people for historical reasons, judging people I've never met and who played no role in the history that shaped my worldview. As in all great stories, a heroine broke my prejudices. She was my host mother.

For the following two years, she crushed my assumptions and stereotypes until one day I was left with gratitude and understanding. To this day, her home is my home. I am hooked! She taught me an uplifting lesson: If you want to disarm someone, love them. We can't connect with the black, white, gay, or Muslim human being standing in the corner until we step into her story. Because let's be real, how dare we expect someone's best self when we are not willing to bring *our* best? To take up my advice, I needed to shatter the language barrier to better engage in American culture.

I looked for help at my school, but they suggested outside help because I was an advanced speaker. So I applied for a tutoring program at the Marathon County Literacy Council. "Maybe that's her," I said to myself every time a woman entered the Marathon County Public Library the day I was supposed to meet my new tutor. Rocking her brown leather boots, she looked at me and said, "Are you Pierre?" On that cold winter evening, Dez became my English tutor and, more importantly, my friend.

Every Wednesday evening, we would meet for a tutoring session. When I murdered English words with my French Creole accent, she patiently waited until I got them right. To this day, I still remember the time she stopped me while I was saying "statistics" to help me pronounce it in a way that didn't sound like "sadistic." Soon, my improvement became as clear as *"Dlo Kokoye"* (coconut water), as we say in Haitian

Creole. A one-year commitment turned into two. We took it one step farther when I challenged myself to blog in English and to join the Wausau Morning Toastmasters where I met Todd Punke, the man who would lead me to have one of my best experiences in the US.

He was driving on the bridge when he looked at me and said, "You should compete."

"Are you out of your mind?" I thought. "I have been in the US for nine months. I barely speak English, and you want me to compete in a Toastmasters impromptu speech contest? Who do you think I am?"

I ignored his comment and let my mind drift in the wondrous beauty of fall expressed through these colorful trees. Suddenly, his voice brought me back: "You will be a good contestant. I can drive you to different locations where you will need to compete."

Todd and I met through the Wausau Morning Toastmasters. He usually picked me up at 6 a.m. every other Thursday to attend the meeting. One day, we even went fishing together in Lake Michigan when I almost caught a fish. With fear nipping at my heels, I took Todd's advice and competed. Despite my misgivings, Todd's encouragement paid off. I won First Place at the Club level, the Area division, the District, and came up third in the state of Wisconsin. In the end, I faced my fears, but this story contained a grander insight: More often than we realize, we need someone to remind us of our gifts. A mentor, a friend, to see the dreams we are afraid to chase. Blinded by our screaming weaknesses, this mentor's mission is to pull us out of the matrix. That is what Todd did for me.

He saw the potential not yet explored in me. He invited me to play in the realm of awesomeness.

When was the last time *your* words stirred someone toward their hidden greatness? Your encouraging words might be just what someone needs to realize they matter. Because everyone matters. Our origin doesn't dictate our potential. No nation has a monopoly on "bad hombre" and no nation has a monopoly on Picassos.

These three experiences shape-shifted my worldview. At their core, they're all stories about the most jubilant human expressions: to love, to teach, and to grow. I could have been a statistic. I was on my way to becoming a radical activist—but others saw David in my eyes. When we give **(insert any group or outcast you want)** a chance, we also give that chance to dozens of people you don't see. When you lean into someone else's story, you acknowledge their humanity. And it's only through these acknowledgments that real bonds are formed.

It's on us to support and empower underdogs. To do this we must first acknowledge them.

1. ACKNOWLEDGE THE UNDERDOGS

I am invisible, understand, simply because people refuse to see me.

— RALPH ELLISON

On a warm thirty-degree Fahrenheit summer day in Wausau, my classmates and I were having our usual talk about life and the world with Chris Knight, the program coordinator of the Scholarship for Education and Economic Development (SEED). I was a member of SEED, and in that room, we had students from El Salvador, Honduras, Mexico, Guatemala, the Dominican Republic, and Haiti. During our intense debate on the state of the world, the coordinator asked, "What do you think is the biggest problem in this world?" We answered famine, hunger, violence, and a lot of different things; everybody was giving their take on the subject. After more than twenty minutes of trying, in his American accent, Chris said, "Indifference. *Indifference is the biggest problem in the world.*" At first, my analytical brain did not want to process that was true, so he continued, "*Even when you have an enemy, at least you acknowledge the enemy, but when you are indifferent, you do not acknowledge.*" The Cambridge dictionary defines "indifference" as a lack of interest in someone or something. When we look right through them, don't notice them, and don't care that we don't notice. When we cannot even see someone, how can we help or work with them?

I don't think the world is purposefully trying to undermine the underdogs. I don't believe in a conspiracy theory that the world is trying to get us. It's a bigger issue than that: we are accustomed to apparent winners, which blinds us from seeing underdogs. We are used to the default. It's difficult for our society to see the ones who are not apparent winners, who are a raw diamond encased in coal. Our minds have clear expectations of the type of human being who make a change, become leaders and social entrepreneurs, but underdogs do not fit these characteristics. We will keep missing out on them unless we learn to identify them and give them the benefit of the doubt that they can bring something of value to this world.

Therefore, the very first step in unleashing innovation at the bottom of the pyramid is to acknowledge the non-obvious winners. We must stop rating and measuring our leaders, winners, champions, dancers, creators, and change-makers on fleeting value and social yardsticks. Because how do you measure love, passion, perseverance, honesty, integrity, or courage? We cannot put a number on these things, but that doesn't mean they are not valuable. We should focus on values like these that cannot be measured. Values such as effort, grit, how they deal with pain, and other characteristics that we know make a good human being. The virtues that make us fall in love, appreciate our parents, build a strong friendship, and so forth. The skills acquired through life experiences are not always visible and are not always valued. They should be *made* visible and they should be more valued. Only then will we be able to empower underdogs.

In your own lives, how many people without a winners' demeanor have you written off because you were looking at the wrong metrics? And how many fools and con artists have we given a platform and supported because they had a winners' demeanor? Is there someone in your life right now whose many disadvantages turn you off? Who's that person? Look in your church and school and businesses. Get to know them to see what they stand for. Look to see if you are not letting your judgment prevent you from seeing a raw diamond. Because underdogs grow up in a world that doesn't see them, it might even be difficult for some of them to know they matter. Until you seek out their values, neither of you might recognize just how much each of you is missing.

2. KEEP THEM ACCOUNTABLE AND FOLLOW UP

In the underdogs' world, threats connected to our existence stifle our attention and cognitive stamina. My biggest social venture failures have been because of a lack of follow up and accountability. While underdog communities and individuals are fighting to change the state of the world they live in, their daily lives pull them in multiple directions, from not eating properly, transportation, family drama, psychological pain, electricity, and other elements which I talked about in Chapter 2. Thus, to make this empowerment sustainable, we need to invest the same amount of time, resources, energy, and money we used to empower them to following up.

Too many projects die the day they launch. The launch becomes the achievement itself when sustainability should be. I believe many great projects attempted by international aid organizations could have been successful if they had invested equal resources and work in the follow-up part of the project. The follow-up should not be an afterthought or just a measurement mechanism but should now become one of the most important parts of the projects. For instance, if you build a computer lab, you need to have spare materials, evaluation mechanisms, trained technicians, and an operational budget for at least two years, giving the lab a fair beginning and helping it get to where it can break even. When applying for funding in the social sector, we are often asked how we plan to ensure the sustainability of the project, but funders would not accept line items in the budget to continue working on a project after launch. For instance, in the business world, we are often advised to have a fund for operating the business for at least a year because it takes three years for most companies to turn a profit. Not allocating funding reasonable for the continuity of a *social* project is a similarly wrong approach for the bottom of the pyramid where material and social infrastructure is broken. It's essential to establish accountability such as mentoring, coaching, project evaluation, psychological evaluation, and providing an adequate level of resources that can keep underdog communities above water so they can continue to breathe and swim toward the ultimate vision.

3. TAKE A CHANCE ON THE NON-OBVIOUS WINNER

Your potential, the absolute best you're capable of—that's the metric to measure yourself against. Your standards are. Winning is not enough. People can get lucky and win. People can be assholes and win. Anyone can win. But not everyone is the best possible version of themselves.

— RYAN HOLIDAY

To fail, you need something to fail *at*, right? The non-obvious winner would only be able to win if they have the opportunity for failure because we all know failure and success are two sides of the same coin. The risk associated with the potential they have is proportionate to the likelihood of failure.

Try to add a few people to your team who are not seen as winners but have the *potential* to win on your team. Do not only give prizes to students with the highest grade but also reward students for their creativity, effort, honesty, and things they excel at. Value excellence in all skills, whether hard or soft. Allow underdogs to fail, because it's not the smartest who should only have this luxury, but the ones who might not take part in the trial and error and disqualify before getting the chance to play. Let them be in the arena and you might be surprised the same way Michael Jordan surprised the world after he did not make the team.

Underdogs are not asking you to let them win; they are asking you to let them play. Only then will the world be able to judge their performance.

4- DEFINE THEM BY THEIR POTENTIAL, NOT THEIR WORST MOMENT

How would you feel if people defined you by your worst behavior? What would you do you if you were defined by the worst act you have ever done? This would not be fair to you, right? Unfortunately, many underdogs have been defined by the one mistake they made, one stupid action. Their life is centered around this one action they cannot go back and change. We ignore everything that they could contribute to society and simply reduce them to a vile failure or inadequacy or embarrassment.

As an ally, we need you to see past our weaknesses and inadequacies as Catherine Hoke did for the prisoners in the program of Defy Ventures, which I describe in the following chapters. There are thousands of people in our community, and many in our own lives, that deserve a second chance. This is what the local organization Fanm Kore Fanm (Women Support Women) did in Haiti in 2019 with its educational program for women composed, for the most part, of sex workers.[67] According to USAID, one in three Haitian women

---

67 (MAXIME 2019)

ages fifteen to forty-nine has experienced physical or sexual violence.[68] Poverty led many young females to become sex workers, one of the most unregulated and marginalized groups in the community, and they are often the victim of violence. Through the two-year program run by Fanm Kore Fanm, the women acquire skills in cosmetology, bakery, and sewing, which help them become independent professionals and possibly, one day, to own a small shop.

Difficulties shook up my will. I was not supposed to do what I am doing if someone's past could dictate their futures. Humans are multidimensional and personalities are fluid. We can become anything we want. The very nature of brain plasticity allows us to unlearn, relearn, and recreate ourselves. Not everybody *will* change, but everybody *can* change. Defining people by their worst actions, behavior, or disadvantages robs them of their humanity and the possibility of becoming better. We can punish them for their worst behavior or reward them for the good they do. Whatever the choice we make, what we water will grow.

CONCLUSION

I fought most of my battles for a bigger purpose. I fought them for the underdogs like myself, the young people with no connection like me, the triers like me. I own my losses but recognize my victories. It's quite possible that I'll never get to see the light at the end of the tunnel, but I want to make sure my life provides footsteps to guide other underdogs through the path I've already walked. That is the spirit that guides

---

68 (United Nations n.d.)

each underdog I have met. It's a desire to give up their lives to open new doors and horizons for others.

Underdog communities and individuals accomplish more when they are empowered than we credit them for. Their empowerment should take into consideration the elements, which we will discuss in Chapter 10. There can be more Rwandas, more Nelson Mandelas, more Abraham Lincolns, more Zozibini Tunzis, more Wright brothers, more Alexandria Ocasio-Cortezes, more Toussaint Louvertures, more William KamKwambas when we acknowledge the underdogs in our lives and communities, define them by their potential not yet explored, and take a chance on the non-obvious winners while keeping them accountable.

CHAPTER SEVEN

THE UNDERDOG ADVANTAGE

UNDERDOG MANIFESTO

The journey will be painful. It will be difficult for others to understand the big vision because you cannot point to a single example in your world. It's often so unrealistic that you cannot even explain it yourself. Willing to die for what you believe will no longer be a metaphor.

You will most likely get depressed from pain overdose. You will cry like a baby at night and rise like a hero during the day. While you're feeling swallowed by your most profound weaknesses, people will still look up to you for strength.

You will be betrayed, judged, vilified, broken, and broke. Most of the time, you will be alone and lonely.

You will miss birthday parties, weddings, and many other events.

Teammates will let you down, and you will need to rise to the occasion.

You will not be allowed to complain. You will often sacrifice your comfort, your family, and your relationships.

You will make a lot of mistakes because you don't know what you are doing. There's no blueprint. You will be forced to improve yourself to adapt to new situations. It's possible you'll die lonely and never see your visions come to life. That's a risk you will have to take. You will be tempted to give up and conform. Parents and family members will mock you for seemingly wasting your time.

Amid all the pain, if you do your work with the best intentions, the gods will reward you. The little impact you have on your environment will fuel your courage. Each person you touch will give you a part of themselves and gratitude will fill your heart. But there's still no guarantee that the big vision will come to life.

You will be asked to give a lot when you have so little. That's the price to pay if you want to advance the human race forward or see your big ideas come to life. In the end, you will find meaning in your sufferings. You will come out as a better human being on the other side if you don't die in the process. Your level of sacrifice will be proportional to your achievement or accomplishment.

For most, life is meant to be enjoyed. And, for those people, you will appear weird. In your heart, you know life is meant to be created, invented, and reorganized. Both philosophies are right; it's just a matter of where you stand on the spectrum.

Because some few have to give their lives so the majority can live. And, you have chosen to be among those few. If you are lucky, you might go down in history as a hero. Or, be forgotten like Nikola Tesla once was.

"*I guess we are not going to eat tonight because there's nothing to cook,*" my mom said to me and my sister eight years ago on a hot summer day in the mountain of Kenscoff. We politely nodded and went straight to bed. While laying on my bed, listening to the disturbing rumbling sound of my belly, I felt a deep sense of rage and I said, "*No, we are not going to sleep like that.*" I went out in the dark found some pinecones in the woods, used a plastic bag to light up the cones to make a fire, and boiled some kazoo that a friend had sent us. This is not something people usually eat boiled alone, but we enjoyed it, laughed about it, and hoped that one day our lives would be better. On that day, I could let my mind go down into hatred and resignation, but then I led it up and out to solutions and dreams.

Living as an underdog goes beyond the material resources that one lacks in order to function in our world. The physical shortfalls are not as important as the mental ones. Underdogs know mentally they are not the first choice, for anyone or anything, and need to put in ten times the effort to get the same output as someone with winner's genes and circumstances. Life comes with certain natural privileges depending on race, social class, and economic background. While we can all be underdogs in different contexts, there are fundamental differences between someone who cannot perform well at some things and someone who is disqualified because of social yardsticks they do not meet or who have been pre-judged on their disadvantages. The former is about someone's inability to perform and the latter is about disqualifying someone because they don't measure up.

Because underdogs have to deal with unique challenges, they develop unique mental tools to help them fulfill their ideals and help their community thrive. Their specific circumstances trained them to come up with a mindset that allows them to continue dreaming for a better life while bathing in inadequacies, insurgencies, and disadvantages. As James Allen beautifully said in his book *As a Man Thinketh*: "*The dreamers are the saviors of the world. As the visible world is sustained by the invisible, so men, through all their trials and sins and sordid vocations, are nourished by the beautiful visions of their solitary dreamers. Humanity cannot forget its dreamers; it cannot let their ideals fade and die; it lives in them; it knows them as the realities which it shall one day see and know.*"

Through countless interviews, discussions, observations, and debate with friends, I have settled on seven elements that help underdogs move past their breaking point and enable them to do and be what they set out to do and be. I called these seven elements the "underdog advantage." Every underdog who has changed his or her life or those around him or her have some combination of these elements. What we call these elements might change and it is often difficult for underdogs to clearly articulate them, but when you dig deeper, the battle comes down to these seven elements.

1. FOUND AN ANCHOR

Convincing themselves that their dreams are possible is the greatest challenge underdogs must overcome to create what they seek to see in the world. For many, poverty can be eating food that expired or not being able to afford a car. My experience of poverty and that of many other Haitian families were not being able to even supply ourselves with the basics. It's very difficult to keep yourself sane when you find yourself in a situation like this, especially when you have a big vision for your life. You often ask yourself if your dreams will ever come true or if you are just delusional.

This act of convincing can be compared to almost a form of violence under which you submit the mind, forcing your mind to accept a pseudo-reality not yet real. The very first thing an underdog does when looking to be or do is look for a grander life mission. They devote their lives to a truth that's bigger than them, a philosophy that supports their beliefs in the potential not yet explored in them. Then they work day in and day out to make the brain accept it as factual reality rather than a crazy thought. It works as an anchor—once the thought becomes integrated into your life, your hope gets restored. An underdogs anchor helps them focus when they feel submerged under inadequacies.

In Maslow's hierarchy of needs, humans start from the basic need for food, water, and sex and move through the other needs until we reach for the highest need: self-actualization. This is not how an underdog operates; they do not go through Maslow's needs in order.

Every underdog I have met or studied in my life has always had their need for realization conflicted with their lesser needs. The sense to bring something to this world compelled her to get involved, volunteer her time, become an activist, or create companies with the potential to change the world. The desire for self-realization weighs more on an emotional scale than the needs for the physiological need for food and water, a sense of belonging, or personal safety.

DEAL WITH PAIN

He who has a why to live can bear almost any how.
— FRIEDRICH NIETZSCHE

To live in an underserved community dominated by struggles and pain requires tunnel vision—a vision that can pull you through the pain to get to the other side.

Underdogs suffer, but in their suffering can often be found their unbreakable capacity. Suffering can cloud our judgment and jail us into our own little world leaving us with only two choices, fight or flight, when there are many variances in the middle of these two extremes. When pain becomes the only prism through which we view life, we play the victim card and accept the reality offered to us. But with a solid "why," underdogs continue to see the potential in themselves and the world around them during intense pain. While they are struggling to eat, they are also thinking about changing the world or leaving a legacy. Underdogs dance in the gray area across the flight and fight spectrum.

Dealing with pain is a necessary wave underdogs must surf to bring innovation to the bottom of the pyramid. Like William Kwakwamba, who continued to build his windmill when his fellow villagers were dying of hunger. On the verge of despair, underdogs see past their pain.

Poverty has taught me resilience, creativity, courage, and most importantly to dream big regardless of circumstances. When you know your inaction will result in you spending the rest of your life in poverty, it creates a sense of urgency. *The time will never be right and the best time is right now.* I am not trying to glamorize poverty, but leveraging it to your advantage is a bet that only the bravest souls can win—the underdogs.

The question is not whether we were born with the right gene but whether we are willing enough to unlearn, relearn, and persevere through the pain until we create the "us" that the world could not see.

3. SWITCH FROM ONE WORLD TO ANOTHER

It was much easier to stand up to the bullies in the playground than to the ones in my head. Convincing yourself that you are here for a grander mission comes down to balancing your current real-life situation with your imaginary life. I called that living in two worlds at once. The best way underdogs manage their sanity is by being flexible. I remember the many times I had to eat something I hated because I couldn't afford better. During these times, my inner critic would kick in to remind me how my life sucked. In this situation, your flexibility of mind comes in very handy. I used to sit at the table using silverware like it was the best meal I'd ever had to calm down my inner critic. Underdogs can acknowledge their current situation (real-life) without letting it define who they are and where they are heading.

While everybody else sees the world in front of them, underdogs can create a whole new world in their minds. They can see the potential not yet explored in themselves while others only see their inadequacies. Children are very good at escaping reality to live in an imaginary world. It's like having a switch in the mind and knowing when to turn it on and off. Underdogs cannot spend too much time in the real world, nor the imaginary one. They cannot become a lunatic without a good grasp of reality nor a bitter realist who is consumed by the pressures of a difficult life.

Underdogs know how to switch from their pain to their potential gain. This emotional agility is one of the secret advantages of an underdog.

4. TURN WHAT'S AVAILABLE INTO THE USEFUL

I do believe that out of adversity comes incredible resourcefulness.

— PHIL KEOGHAN

Some jobs and tools only exist in a country like Haiti. Do you know why? Because we did not find what's available in the rich countries, so we use what's available to us. When operating in a scarce environment, the choices we have become limited. Faced with this limitation, we need to ask ourselves: What's available here? What do I have as a resource? Which one will cost no money? Which one costs less? Which one can I afford? Which one do I have the skills and the manpower to transform into my desired outcomes? Which one can I transform the fastest?

Underdogs do not just practice surface-level thinking by adopting the solutions closest to them or that come first in their minds. They are willing to be uncomfortable for a moment to dig deeper to find the most unconventional and creative solutions. Before asking for help and more resources, they undergo an inventory of all resources available in their immediate environment.

Dancing and music are ingrained into the Haitian tradition. Even motorcycle taxis play music, so instead of buying speakers from China, some people with no formal education in music or sounds used PVC tubes to create their own motorcycle speakers. When the Congolese music collective KOKOKO! could not afford to buy musical instruments in Kinshasa, they decided to create their own instruments of kitchen pots, tin cans, and air conditioner parts, and now they are touring all over the world still using junk to make music and knocking on people's consciousness to, as they said, *"open up to the kind of musical innovation we're proposing."* [69]

5. CHALLENGE THE STATUS QUO

A certain level of delusion is necessary. One of the key characteristics of an underdog is the ability to believe in the impossible. The belief that there's something different that can be done. This belief pushes underdogs to try harder and come up with unconventional solutions to conventional problems.

Underdogs are rebels, they do not accept the current state of a thing and don't want to conform. A sense of rebellion against the status quo is one of the most recognizable traits of underdogs. They rebel against the people closest to them,

---

69 (SARMIENTO 2019)

their mothers and fathers, to make their visions come to life. They are not afraid of showing some disagreeableness which is one of the traits of the Big Five personalities theory.[70] Psychological scientists Samuel Hunter of Pennsylvania State University and Lily Cushenbery of New York University at Stony Brook note that new ideas are often met with greater skepticism and criticism than conventional ones so people willing to be disagreeable are needed to argue and fight for their ideas in the face of criticism. They may end up being more successful in actually getting their ideas implemented.[71] When the status quo rejects underdogs, they aren't willing to leave without a fight. Exactly what William Kwamkwamba did when he confronted his father with his group of friends to force him to give the bike wheel to create a windmill.

When someone has a new idea, most people who hear it will disapprove. My favorite author, Seth Godin, called it the "Gulf Of Disapproval."¹ If we keep track of all the people who don't like our ideas and who won't support us, it's most likely we will give up. That's why it is important to track the blue lines instead; the few early adopters who are willing to support our new idea and vision.[72] Underdogs persist to create value for people, which compounds over time. As they grow their supporters one by one, only then can they start influencing the ones who did not accept them.

The current state of affairs is not working to their advantage, so they are compelled to change it.

---

70 (Psychology Today n.d.)
71 (Science 2015)
72 (Godin 2016)

6. HAVE PASSION

"Follow your passion" has become a cliché lacking real essence. More and more people are saying it without really knowing the true meaning. What is passion? For a long time, we have been fooled into thinking passion is doing something easy, something we love that doesn't require a big sacrifice or high discipline. In other words, just a hobby, but is that what passion is? Let's take a look at the Latin root of the word. Passion is from the Latin verb "pati," which means "to suffer." It's why, in Christianity, the period of Jesus' suffering is called Christ's passion.

I believe when you are on the right path, you will face trials and setbacks. Underdogs are passionate people who are willing to accept the full package. Guided by their love for their work, they invest their souls in solving problems that affect their fellow human beings. Above all, underdogs love what they do and are willing to suffer to be and do what they love. They are not guided by the social benefits and financial gains of their change. They are driven by an immense passion for the transformational process.

7- ADAPT TO UNCONVENTIONAL SITUATIONS

Microsoft lost the war against Apple.

Kodak could not adapt, and now they are out of business.

To adapt means to evolve and respond instead of reacting. Analyze what's in front of us to discover what type of person we need to be to face the challenge or new situation head-on. To paraphrase Charles Darwin: "*It is not the strongest of the species that survives, nor the most intelligent that survives. It is the one that is the most adaptable to change."*

Disruption does not only happen in the tech world but it also happens in our own lives, and underdogs have learned to adapt in order to survive. They keep their vision but are willing to change tactics.

The best advice I've ever received came from an Indian MBA student. His profound insight has changed the way I've looked at life and business ever since.

I was working on a business plan for an entrepreneurship contest and he said to me, in his Indian accent, "Stanley, you know you can always pivot your idea, right?" I look at him with a confused look. Then, he went on to explain that if we turn a coffee mug multiple times, people who are looking will see a different outline of that mug each time we turn it. Like a coffee mug, an idea has multiple faces and you can change the face of an idea without changing the core idea itself. What he called a "pivot."

Underdogs don't have to change who they are at their core but can change the way they carry themselves in the world. At any time, without invitation, change might come into your life, and improving our ability to cope with change will lead the way to a happier and richer life. It will come when you are unprepared. It will come when we want to take a break. It will come when we wish to settle. Viktor Frankl spent years in a Nazi concentration camp and survived without letting the situation suck his soul. He said that he would know when his fellow prisoners were about to die or go crazy. They would stop taking showers, stop showing up on time, stop following the rules of the camp, and stop shaving. They stopped adapting and accepted the situation as normal.[73] Underdogs, on the other hand, are the ultimate adaptation machine.

CONCLUSION

Talented or not, these advantages guide the underdogs who make it despite the odds. Talent without constant practice is a wasted gift. Constant practice with the right strategy and mental tools gives birth to impactful change-makers, leaders, and entrepreneurs. Constant effort creates Michael Jordan, the light bulb, and black freedom.

I know how hard it is to keep running the race when the stadium inside is booing. Shaking, fearful, often with tears in their eyes, underdogs will stand in the field; fighting and slaying the dragons of poverty, pain, and insufficiency as many times as they show up. Because they know: their best is on the other side of their fears. The battle is not outside of them. They don't leave their fate in the hands of the system, nor the status quo. If they hedge, they lose their edge.

---

73 (Frankl 1946)

CHAPTER EIGHT

HUMANITY AT THE CENTER OF INNOVATION

The people who need design ingenuity the most, the poorest 90 percent of the global population, have historically been deprived of it.

— ALICE RAWSTHORN

In their quest to save the world, the humanitarian community can often become the ones at the center of the change that needs to be enacted. Instead of working with the underdogs and being the catalyst for innovation, we often become the inappropriate center of innovation by leaving out the necessary partnership with the person we seek to serve.

Experts are often detached from the people they are looking to serve. They become far removed from the community and unable to put themselves in their shoes. They see them not as human beings but as study subjects. People are not just a data set. Considering the human emotions and aspirations in people we want to help is crucial to creating innovation that satisfies the real needs of the community or market.

After carefully analyzing the weaknesses of my entrepreneurship education program for high school students, I was looking for a better solution. A solution that doesn't simply *teach* the kids but involves them. This is where the idea to change the program format into a product creation camp came to us. In July 2016, we created the InovAction camp—a nine-day program that convenes underprivileged youth to create or re-invent a commodity product. The students were divided into four different groups: Branding, Budget and Financing, Ideation, and Marketing. Each group was attached to a coach (graphic designer, videographer, product designer, etc.) who served as a guide while they went on their quest to reinvent an old product.

That summer, we asked them to reinvent peanut butter and make something wild in every aspect of it. Throughout the camp, they learned about branding, then created a brand and ad for their product, and gave it a cool name (Kens, short for their city name Kenscoff). On the ninth day, they presented three different versions of peanut butter. One based on pineapple and honey, one with grape, and one based on Rhum Barbancourt. We organized a tasting party where we collected rave reviews. It was so good that it was no longer peanut butter but cool-chocolate type things. Besides the beautiful products, what surprised us the most was their tagline "*Le copain du pain*," which rhymes and means "the friend of the bread" in French. At that moment, I realized that some kids who've never heard about branding or product creation could come up with such cool concepts and that creativity was not foreign to anybody, as explained in Chapter 3. This is where I learned what it means to turn cheerleaders on the sidelines into players.

I've always been taught you can manage projects, but you cannot manage people. Over the years, I have also realized that you cannot save the world unless you save people. In fact, in trying to accomplish our boldest dreams to move humanity forward, we often forget humanity is made of humans; humans with stories, pain, failures, desires, weaknesses. Trying to solve humanity's problems while seeing the world as a concept evolves our philosophical worldview by leaving the majority behind. Many people and organizations are trying their best to help the BOP get out of survival mode and we are grateful to have them as an ally. If you are on such a quest, I truly hope you will put humanity first, as Nobel Peace Prize Laureate Muhammad Yunus and the founders of the Ubongo project did.

PARTICIPATION ACTION RESEARCH

The majority of the solutions to poverty or to increase the quality of life are based on traditional research. Researchers come to Haiti and many other countries to study our poverty. They spend time researching then come up with data points that are published months or years later in a language mostly understood by other academics who often use them for other research projects. This data is not always accessible to the countries where the studies were done and people who live at the BOP and are trying to change their community are unaware of the scientific evidence. I think it's fair to demand that communities or countries participating in a study have access to these findings. Research is often the job of the experts, but what if we could engage the people we seek to understand in the research process? This is exactly what the research method named "Participation Action Research" advocates: research that matches with actions.

As the name suggests, Participation Action Research is a research methodology that tries to understand the world and change it at the same time through experiments and the involvement of the affected communities. In this method, communities aren't simply passive data providers. They also participate in collecting, interpreting, and reacting to the data in a timely manner.[74]

After Muhammad Yunus returned to Bangladesh in 1976 as the Professor and Head of the Rural Economics Program at the University of Chittagong, he wanted to find a way to help the poor get access to loans. He approached the banks and many other financial institutions, but they did not want to embark on this journey with him. Their main concern was that the poor were insolvent and were not going to be able to pay back the loan. So Yunus decided to launch an Action Research Project of designing a credit system to provide banking services to the rural poor.

After the action research demonstrated its success in Jobra (a village adjacent to Chittagong University) and some of the neighboring villages, the central bank of the country and other the nationalized commercial banks got on board and supported the project to be done in other communities. In October 1983,

---

74   (Vera Institute 2016)

the Grameen Bank Project became an independent bank owned by the rural poor who have 90 percent of its shares, while the remaining 10 percent is owned by the government.

Had he conducted normal research, we would not have Grameen Bank today and the many lives changed through Grameen Bank microloans would not have benefitted. While there's more work to be done, I am positive that this type of action research project has a more positive impact on a community than the normal ones. Having met the Nobel Prize Laureate and listening to him telling the Grameen Bank story, I wonder why we don't continue to use this model if it's successful?

HUMAN-CENTERED DESIGN

I met Tom Adamson in 2016 through the Acumen Plus platform when he was looking for other people in Haiti who were also taking the Storytelling for Change course. After this course, we gathered a group of three professionals to take additional courses and meet every Wednesday to discuss them. Everything changed after we took this Human-Centered Design course. I was familiar with design thinking through Tom Kelley's book *Creative Confidence* but did not realize the power of human-centered design until I took this one class. Human-Centered Design was my ticket to better projects, work, and events.

Human-centered design is a thinking process and a creative approach to solving problems that put great emphasis on the human or people we seek to serve.[75] Using human-centered

---

75 (IDEO n.d.)

design means putting ourselves in the shoes of people we seek to serve by living in their environment, interviewing them, and experiencing their lives. Empathy is a core component of this methodology that consists of three phases. In the *Inspiration* phase, we learn from people we seek to serve by immersing in their experiences and daily lives. Following the inspiration comes the *Ideation* phase where we start designing and prototyping solutions that take into account the elements we'd gathered in the Inspiration phase. Finally, in the *Implementation* phase, we bring these solutions to the market to get feedback, iterate what we've done, and constantly refine the solution.

For instance, the design revolution called D-Rev is a nonprofit that puts the human at the center of their innovation process. Their mission is to design products that serve customers who live on less than $4 a day to improve their health and increase their income.

Mild jaundice occurs in about 60 percent of full-term newborn babies and up to 80 percent of premature babies. In many developing countries, children born into poverty suffer severe consequences due to delayed or inadequate treatment, and hospitals cannot afford phototherapy devices or often replace them with wrong lights. After countless field trips, instead of inventing a new device, D-Rev redesigned one that already exists, adapting it to the market they seek to serve and making it affordable. D-Rev managed to design a phototherapy device costing $400 while similar devices cost around $3,500. *"We learned early on when testing prototypes with users, that we shouldn't radically shake up how phototherapy is normally done,"* says Nicole Rappin, D-Rev

Operations Manager. After developing the first version of the device in 2012 from users' feedback, they came up with a better version in 2014.[76]

Profit is not a substitution for social impact, but companies can still make a profit by putting the market at the center of the innovation process. Pushing products to the base of the pyramid is no longer a good strategy for sustainable growth. We must design a solution that incorporates feedback from the community we serve.

TURNING THE PYRAMID UPSIDE DOWN
When people visit underserved countries, they often do "charity purchases," which are the act of buying an item out of pity for the creators or the products' sellers. To create a thriving bottom of the pyramid, we need our creators to be competitive and create products and services that can compete with imported ones as well as satisfy the physical needs and emotional needs of the market. That's why it's important to integrate design thinking courses everywhere at the BOP (schools, churches, colleges, public markets) to help creators come up with solutions that the world wants instead of solutions people are guilted to donate to, buy from, or support.

Charity purchase will continue at the BOP as long as these local creators do not have access to training, tools, and market savvy to help them create refined and standardized products that can compete with imported fashion, food, and craft products. Because of these issues, the competition in creating

---

76 (IDEO n.d.)

low-quality products is high and these entrepreneurs can barely survive on what they are selling. Even local people will purchase imported products instead of local ones, as I have seen many times in Haiti. That's why, in 2020, we are organizing a "Buying Local" market every month at our workshare space and also on social media so people everywhere can continue to buy local while we design a co-creation space for entrepreneurs to refine their products. Design thinking and co-creating labs can turn charity products and services into products that local and international buyers long for.

Ubongo Kids, a Tanzania-based social enterprise, does this very well through its online platform that provides education and entertainment to six million kids across Africa. The *Ubongo Kids* platforms (radio, websites, apps, TV shows) provide financial literacy, encourage a growth mindset, and offer an introduction to coding, all these through TV shows, animated series, and catchy original songs. The *Ubongo Kids'* mission is to transform learning for the 440 million kids in Africa through localized edutainment on accessible technologies to help kids learn, and then leverage their learning to change their lives. *Ubongo Kids* reach over 6.4 million East African households monthly, without counting hundreds of thousands of other kids who are accessing content on the internet. All of this started with a $3,000 award received from Fire Africa Award in 2017.[77]

With mass manufacturing capable of producing millions of the same products quickly, I predict the BOP will hold a great competitive advantage in the market of the future if they can

---

77 (UBONGO KIDS 2018)

create creatively-produced, original, and well-designed products. Why do I say that? When everything we buy becomes a commodity and mass-produced, we would want to be, to look like, and to buy something extraordinary. And if the BOP is focusing on craftsmanship and design, we will be the artists of the new renaissance. As machines become the norm, people will start looking for what's humanely produced, and because we at the BOP are not machines we will be able to thrive while adopting only on technology that amplifies the impact we have in the world. Turning the innovation pyramid upside down is not simply about big companies selling to the four billion people at the BOP, it's the reverse. It's millions of people in the BOP selling to the other three billion people at the top.

CONCLUSION

In our quest to solve the world's greatest challenges, we need to remember to put humanity first. The problems we are trying to solve aren't concepts, they are the dire elements that are wrecking millions of lives daily. Solving problems at the BOP is not like solving a math challenge or a coding challenge; it's like playing with fire. Because millions of lives are at stake.

This is to say that, when designing policies or stimulating the underdogs to innovate, it should always be in the interest of humanity. It's funny how we want to conquer Mars, but we are still unable to improve the lives of billions living at the bottom of the pyramid. Such great pride every time a new rocket goes to space, yet little applause when humanity shows compassion and moves some of the BOP upward.

There are tools out there to help us think and act while considering humanity. While they are often difficult to adopt, they have been effective on many fronts. If tools like human-centered design and participatory action research are producing results on a small scale, we ought to scale them to large samples. The important thinking models or innovative ways to approach a problem should not stay at Stanford University so that a few can be seen as superheroes when they put them to good use. They need to be democratized to the lower base at the pyramid so that underdogs who are unable to move higher with the tools available to them can use these to transform their lives and the lives of other fellows.

PART THREE

ENACTING THE UNDERDOG REVOLUTION

CHAPTER NINE

UNLEASHING INNOVATION AT THE BOTTOM OF THE PYRAMID

―

If you look at history, innovation doesn't come just from giving people incentives; it comes from creating environments where their ideas can connect.

— STEVEN JOHNSON

Gross Domestic Product (GDP) growth doesn't mean that more people are getting richer or improving their quality of life; it may just mean people at the top are getting richer. Economists and big experts keep focusing on numbers like Genome Database (GDB) as a sign of progress when these numbers don't do justice to people living at the bottom of the pyramid. Research by the former Chief Economist of the World Bank, François Bourguignon, found:

> "It is not the inequality of economic outcomes, income, or consumption, per se that hinders economic development but other dimensions of economic and social inequality, including family background, access to the credit market, education, health care, security, justice, and so-called 'horizontal' inequality between ethnic groups or gender. It turns out that the inequality of income, on which the empirical literature focuses almost exclusively, is a very imperfect marker of this broader definition of inequality, that corresponds to the inequality of opportunity."

This is to say that we cannot simply focus on economic growth if we want the BOP to thrive. We need to address some of the underlying inequality as mentioned in Chapter 7 about leveling the playing field.[78]

Teacher: "William Kamkwamba. Stand up."

Kamkwamba: "My father will pay, sir."

Teacher: "You are stealing from the family of every remaining student in is school."

Kamkwamba: "My father will pay, sir."

Teacher: "You're stealing from myself and from every member of faculty."

Kamkwamba: "My father will pay."

---

78 (Bourguignon 2015)

Teacher: "You're expelled from Kachokolo, and you will never be allowed to study here again or any school in this district. Collect your things and go."

This is one of the most touching scenes of the movie *The Boy Who Harnessed The Wind*,[79] based on the real-life experiences of William Kamkwamba.

Born on August 5, 1987, in Dowa, Malawi, William Kamkwamba grew up on his family farm in Masitala Village, Wimbe, two and a half hours northeast of Malawi's capital city. He's the second eldest of six children.

Famine was ravaging the town and his father could no longer afford to pay his eighth-grade school fees. Forced to drop out, he spent five years unable to go to school. During this time, the junkyard became the playground where William collected junk he could transform into useful objects. While he could not continue to access the class, he found a way to sneak into the school library. He would spend his time reading books above his grade level until one day he stumbled upon a book named *Using Energy* written by Mary Atwater, the book that sparked his interest in building a windmill. In this book, William learned about dynamo, wind power, and other mind-blowing science discoveries.

The drought was getting worse. People were dying. Things were so hard that his father had to sell the metal sheets of his house to get money to buy food. Based on what he learned

---

[79] (Ejiofor 2019)

from the book, William wanted to build a windmill and water pump using materials he found in the junkyard. As appeared in a *Wired* article in February 2009, "He experimented with a small model using a cheap dynamo and eventually made a functioning wind turbine that powered a small radio."[80] Following that small success, he knew he had proof of the concept that he could build bigger. His friend went to the junkyard to continue collecting trash and help him build a bigger windmill that powered a radio, phone, and some other small appliances. After, a local newspaper wrote about it and William was invited to share his stories at TEDx Global Stage in 2007. His detractors became supporters, and word soon got out about his invention. He became an inspiration for people living at the BOP and all over the world.

I remember seeing Kwamkwamba speaking in Stevens Point, Wisconsin, in March 2013 and thinking, "*Wow, this is an incredible story that we all need to know.*" After his speech, we met at his signing booth and talked about life and what we think we can do to change things in our respective countries. From this point forward, I knew that we can have more William Kwamkambas if we inspire people at the BOP to innovate.

When people talk about ways to bring innovation in underserved communities, it's either "we saved them from their pain using the charity model" or "we milk the cow by using them in a for-profit progressive way." The first option is about giving handouts and the culture of seeing the ones at the bottom as incapable and, as many used to say, "lazy." The latter is opening the market to multinational businesses to

---

80 (Zetter 2009)

create low-paying jobs or using models such as pay-as-you-go to turn the BOP into a market, a model that's painful for the BOP customers, as coined by the well-known behavioral economist, Dan Ariely.[81] In my research, I have not yet found a holistic approach or method that puts the person we seek to serve at the center of the innovation process as co-researchers and co-creators.

In 2019 alone, more than ten countries, including Chile, Spain, Lebanon, Ecuador, Iraq, Haiti, and Hong Kong have protested against social inequality. Many of these countries we have previously considered emerging economies and an economic model to follow now have their populations on the street demanding a more fair and equal living. For instance, Chile is one of the wealthiest of Latin America's countries and yet they have the worst levels of income equality among the thirty-six member nations of the Organization for Economic Co-operation and Development (OECD).[82] When the economy is growing each quarter in Haiti that doesn't mean my mother who was earning $50 a month as a teacher is getting a raise. We at the BOP don't understand these GDP numbers and could not care less. What we know is our daily human experience is tainted by sickness, trash, inequality, poor education, and lack of resources. The world should stop trying to *lift* people out of poverty and start creating conditions for people to *raise themselves* out of poverty. Given the failed attempts of the top-to-bottom innovation approach, I am advocating for a new model. I am advocating for a bottom-up approach where people affected by these issues are at the center and

---

81 (Duke University - The Fuqua School of Business 2013)

82 (BBC News 2019)

forefront of the innovation think tank as thinkers, innovators, and co-researchers, and not case studies or data providers. What enables people at the top to innovate has nothing to do with special powers. It all comes down to mental models, tools, design thinking, and knowledge. What would happen if we provided the right *thinking* framework to people at the BOP? We'd empower them with tools to ideate, prototype and test their innovative solutions. So let's transform ghettos into living innovation hubs and thinking labs.

Throughout my research, I have found interesting data about innovation, creativity, and the power of design. Based on my view of the world, my research, and more than twenty years' experience in poverty, I have come up with a three-step process I call the "Underdog Innovation Model," which I believe would enable underserved communities to thrive and underdogs to create growth. My ultimate goal in this chapter is to present to you my theory on how to unleash innovation at the bottom of the pyramid and also introduce you to other existing working models that we could also apply on top of my propositions. These are open-source ideas that I invite you to build upon and reframe. I am not here to protect my writer's ego.

STEP 1: WASTE AND ASSETS INVENTORY
If you don't patch the hole, more resources will not fill the tank. When we think about underserved communities, it's easy to forget that they also have resources even when they are not explored or not abundant. Before we can decide to help out a community within the BOP, we need to understand their waste-to-resources ratio. For example, if we seek to bring

innovation in the health sector to a difficult community, we need to do an inventory of resources already available in the medical field in this community. Maybe it's not as modern as we intend it to be, but is there any existing solutions already provided? How do people in this community solve those problems? Are there any medicinal plants they use? What are those?

People at the BOP are not sitting there dying and not doing anything. They are constantly thinking about ways to extend their lives or to improve the quality of their lives. So they come up with their own ways to deal with a specific problem. Maybe it's not as effective as we eventually want, but it clearly helps them and we need to understand the underlying cultural elements that make those choices ideal for this community. While identifying assets available, we should also look at the waste (or threats) that affect this particular group of the sector we seek to innovate with. We need to do a proper map of human resources, material resources, financial resources, and cultural resources that are being wasted in every sector or market we seek to serve.

Croix Des Beaux Sales, or Croix Des Bossales, an ancient market where they used to sell slaves in Haiti, is now the biggest public market in Port au Prince. Farmers and *Madan Sara* (women sellers) come from all over Haiti to sell in this market, each part named after a big city of Haiti. As I mentioned earlier in the book, Haiti imports $3.618 billion and exports $980.2 million—a pretty terrible imbalance.[83] Every day when you pass by this market, you would find a lot of

---

83 (Central Intelligence Agency n.d.)

agricultural products that are going to waste because of a lack of a way to conserve them. At the same time, people in Cité Soleil in the same city are dying of hunger. We keep asking for foreign aid and we keep importing from the Dominican Republic. Unless we change our ability to preserve agricultural products, improving our yield from the earth will still just lead to rotting vegetables. We need systems that can help us reduce losses. That would be a BOP solution.

REDUCING WASTE AUTOMATICALLY INCREASES RESOURCES

We need to address waste and efficiency in underserved communities. We need to find where resources are being wasted because of inadequate management systems. We need to identify this wastebasket because we cannot keep pouring resources into a wastebasket that has so many holes. In many underserved communities and countries around the world, countless resources like food, medical supplies, empty government houses, money, human resources, and so on are being wasted because of inefficient management.

Only by knowing our strengths and weaknesses can we properly identify opportunities that we can create or solutions we can come up with. After identifying the waste, we need to identify the reason behind the waste and the local innovators behind solutions that already exist. In the public sector, many processes are broken and it takes an enormous amount of time to perform simple tasks. We need to identify roadblocks, bottlenecks, and corruption, and work actively to resolve them before we can bring any type of innovation that can bring transformative change on a large scale. There's this famous

Haitian saying, "*Mwen ap kode ap dekode*," meaning there's no use tying one part of the knot when others are untying the other part.

While the world is looking for ways to reduce the use of plastic straws, there are local innovators in Haiti who are already creating bamboo straws.[84] Maybe you would say that's not scalable. If by scalable you mean producing one million in a machine every day, probably not. But imagine how many people in the developing world could start producing this instead of working in inhumane factories for large corporations.

STEP 2: REWARD LOCAL INNOVATORS AND CREATORS

Did you know that in Haiti there's a guy who builds beautiful, highly functional buses for public transportation?[85] He has already built more than four buses and they're perfect for what Haitians need and want. He's still an ignored element in Haiti; the government doesn't care and the public sector doesn't care, and international figures haven't acknowledged him either. How can we expect the BOP to grow when local innovators are not rewarded? Human behavior is about actions and rewards. Rewarding local innovators is the best way to encourage others to innovate and come up with great solutions.

There are prisons to punish people who break the law and who destroy society. Is there a place for people who create good or actively try to bring change? How do we reward these people?

---

84 (AJ+ 2019)

85 (Flecher 2018)

Over half of the population of Tanzania lacks internet access. That's the challenge Given Edward is solving in Tanzania with Mtabe, an artificial intelligence-powered SMS platform and app which delivers educational content to students without internet access, pricey smartphones, or even textbooks.[86] Many local innovators are already in the field trying to bring solutions to the problems they see. Edward and others are being rewarded for their work and it's important to reward these local innovators we discover based on the first step, the Inventory. Here are three ways we reward them:

- Training—In the *Inventory* process, you found someone has been using medicinal plants that are effective to cure sickness. We must ensure we help this person to enhance his or her skills through online training, scholarships, books, mentors, or internships that will allow them to broaden their horizons and make what they do better.

- Visibility—There's not a worse pain than doing your best and not get recognized for your work. Everybody wants to be useful and important. So the local governments and international organizations should organize events and ways to make these local innovators feel important to their community. In doing so, they will want to continue to live and create for their community. For instance, 85 percent of Haitian college graduates are working abroad, as compared to 5 percent of educated Indians or Chinese.[87] When local creators don't come back to the community, others don't see the need to stay.

---

86 (Quartz 2019)

87 (Wasti 2018)

- Funding—I am not talking about cash for a project, I am talking about funding for themselves. I'm talking about selling a product or a service. When local creators receive the cash, they will likely invest in themselves, new materials, or resources to become better at what they do.

If small creators are not rewarded, fewer people will continue working in their home communities. When I was a kid, in a village called Nouvelle-Touraine, almost all the people were involved in agriculture. Now most of them have stopped farming because it did not give them a better life. Today most young people no longer farm because there is no reward. They went to the city to become *potè* (laborers carrying goods for money) rather than working for no reward.

When a nurse comes back to an underserved community, her skills are not wasted like a lot of people might think. In every community, there are a few people working hard to bring value back in spite of the lack of resources. But we need to encourage more people to come back. Local governments and the aid organizations and investors should try to identify the people who come back and reward them for their work, so more people would want to come back to build with their communities. Because every community has a role to play in making the world a better place.

STEP 3: SCALE LOCAL MARKET VALIDATED SOLUTIONS

The word "scale" is often associated with machines rather than humans, but that's not the definition of scale. If there's a resource the BOP has in quantity, it is people. Labor is not as costly as in other countries, even with a substantial pay increase. The scaling mode for the BOP should be based on human capital first. We can't go straight to robots when the majority of the population of these communities have never worked in their entire life. This would only widen the divide between rich and poor, educated and uneducated.

After identifying resources, waste, and rewarding local creators, it's essential to scale solutions that work. When local solutions need improvement, we can have two courses of actions:

Selling innovative ideas to large companies to continue the innovation process and come back to test the final solutions, then commercialize it or apply it in the sector in which they seek to innovate.

Invest in local entrepreneurs to develop the final solutions and bring them to the market.

If a local solution is market-validated, we need local Angel Investors and social venture capitalists willing to take the risk to make funding available. Funding from people in the diaspora can also be available to allow the diaspora of a community or country to invest in scalable local social ventures or business ventures.

Call me an idealist, but I dream of ghettos turning into innovation labs. How do we do that? Think tanks can be created in each ghetto for people to come up with ideas about the problems their community faces. Besides all the different recommendations I made earlier, this would be the most effective in my view.

CROWDSOURCING

The crowd holds immense power and wisdom when we decide to tap into their genius. We can witness their power in the process of crowdsourcing in which individuals or organizations acquire ideas, finances, local services, and services from a large public, mostly internet users, to solve problems and innovate. The same way politicians ask people to vote for them during an election, what if, when elected, they could also crowdsource for ideas, funding, effort, and mindset to help the community solve their issues?

Khan Academy uses the down-top innovation by allowing instructors to create over 3,000 classes in science and math that have been viewed over 200 million times and cost zero dollars to the students. With their flexible model that allows users to give feedback that instructors can use to refine lessons, this is a vivid example of the bottom-up approach.

Quirky has a user base of 354,000 users who are inventors. They pay a ten-dollar fee to submit product ideas and can also rate and influence others' product branding, product development, and all phases of a product. Already, 300 products have been created through the platform, which are sold through Amazon, Target, and many other retailers in the United States.[88]

Author Nancy Gibbs, former Managing Editor for *TIME* magazine said: "*We know what the birth of a revolution looks like: A student stands before a tank. A fruit seller sets himself on fire. A line of monks links arms in a human chain.*

---

88 (Caldbeck 2013)

Crowds surge, soldiers fire, gusts of rage pull down the monuments of tyrants, and maybe, sometimes, justice rises from the flames. It doesn't have to happen only when justice rises, we can harness the power of the crowd for innovation, creativity, and much more."[89] Outside of the realm of politics, the crowd is still powerful and by not tapping into their genius, we are persisting in believing the normal stereotype: The BOP is looking for a savior.

HUMANISTIC ENTERPRISE AND CREATIVE-CAPITALISM

From Bill Gates to Marc Benioff to Brunello Cucinelli, I believe the richest of the world have a bigger role to play in redefining new ways of doing business, a new way of gaining and managing wealth. Call it creative-capitalism[90] as Bill Gates did or name it humanistic enterprise[91] as Brunello Cucinelli did, we can all agree we need our billionaires to be active players in the creation of the Underdog Revolution. We need billionaires who have profited from the unequal system to be allied in fixing it. To do this, we can't put them out or label them as the enemy. We need to keep them accountable through laws and regulations. With their wealth and reach, they can either push the BOP into more trouble or foster an environment for underdogs to lift themselves.

I am not advocating for billionaires to give us money, I am advocating that the richest pay their fair share the same way

---

89 (Gibbs 2011)

90 (Koehn 2008)

91 (CUOFANO n.d.)

we expect the poor to stop asking for a handout and not be dependent on government help.

When a company pays workers low wages, that should not be tolerated. For example, the Workers Consortium Rights state in a 2013 report the following: *"Several brands producing in Haiti, including Gildan Activewear and Fruit of the Loom, have committed to remedying both current and past non-compliance with the minimum wage. However, Caracol's buyers have not made any commitment to ensure that the factory complies with the minimum wage."* We regulate the poor and put them in jail when they break the law. Half of the world's prison population of about 9 million is held in the United States, China, or Russia. The same laws that work for the vulnerable should also work for the rich.

Nobody becomes rich alone. We all benefit from the community we live in. Giving back to the community, therefore, is not a favor but a duty. Giving back doesn't mean a handout, it also means decent jobs, social improvements, and less abuse of power. Making the world a better place makes Gates look good and also satisfies his need for self-actualization, which is the highest need in Maslow's Hierarchy of Needs. Not making the world a better place doesn't only make it bad for the poor. With no other hope, immigrants fleeing hopelessness will come flooding in from everywhere and crime will rise because when injustice prevails, we only look out for ourselves and see others as the enemy we need to destroy.

Charity is not the only way to interact with the most vulnerable. This is exactly what I am trying to preach in this book. As humans, we live in interdependence. What if workers no longer work? We each have a role to play in each other's' well-being and we must play it to ensure a better world for us and our children. It's in our own self-interest.

Wage theft in the Haitian apparel industry was a subject of a report [92] that had the following conclusion and reinforces my point about accountability: *"The significant wage theft represented by these minimum wage violations has devastating effects on workers' families. Even when these families forgo adequate nutrition and medical care, they remain trapped in a cycle of debt from borrowing money to cover the costs of basic survival. North American brands and retailers have benefited in the form of low prices from their suppliers from the systematic theft of wages from some of the poorest workers in the Western Hemisphere. In order to prevent further harm to these workers and their families, these brands and retailers have the responsibility to ensure that their Haitian supplier factories can and do comply with the legal minimum wage and make workers whole for all the earnings of which they have been unlawfully deprived."* Although this report came in 2013, according to a survey of 2019 by Solidarity Center, the daily minimum wage of $5.07 is more than four times less than their cost of living for export apparel workers.[93]

The Italian designer Brunello Cucinelli's work in Solomeo is the finest example of what can happen when billionaires play their roles. Many little towns in Italy are being deserted, but the village of Solomeo is thriving due to the business philosophy of Cucinelli. While Brunello Cucinelli's clothing is

---

92 (Worker Rights Consortium 2013)

93 (L. Stewart 2019)

designed for the wealthiest, he donates 20 percent of its profits and creates a human work environment for his employees that many companies in Silicon Valley want to emulate. He restored old buildings, paid workers way more than the rest of the market, and created conditions for them to be creative.[94] We'll discuss more about his story in Chapter 11. According to the Wealth-X Billionaire Census, there are 2,604 billionaires in the world and 47 million millionaires according to the global wealth report of 2019.[95] It's an impressive number of people that we cannot ignore if we truly want to unleash innovation at the BOP. We cannot solve injustice by injustice, and justice doesn't mean doing injustice to the ones who may or may not be victims of it. We cannot take their wealth away because the current system allowed them to get rich, but what we can do is work with them as allies to fix that system for a better world in which inequality is not the norm and wealthy people are not demonized.

UNLEASHING INNOVATION AT THE BOP
Turning the pyramid upside down is about introducing folks to design thinking and waiting to see what they come up with. Turning the pyramid upside down is leveling the playing field by giving people access to valuable information and setting up an environment favorable for the apparent winners as well as for the non-obvious winners.

Unleashing innovation at the BOP is doing like CoCread, a program that enables girls in the slums in Haiti to become

---

94 (CUOFANO n.d.)
95 (Wealyh X 2019)

coders. Turning the pyramid upside down is introducing our people to Arduino. It's opening financial opportunities with platforms like PayPal to weaker nations. It's giving a Bible as well as a Chromebook.

CONCLUSION

We can continue trying to save the BOP or we can finally decide to empower them to save themselves.

The BOP can produce much more than poverty, gangs, and mediocrity. We are rich in human resources, rich in dreams, and all we need is for the world to believe in us, to trust us, and support us as if we were capable of lifting ourselves because we can. If we were not creative, most of us would be dead already. But every day millions of underdogs are getting in the street to sell, to teach, to create, to demand a better life because we believe we need a better us. Do you know what people in the BOP who don't have anything do to survive? They help each other and organize themselves in a way that allows the other to still live and fight for another day.

Innovation is happening on a small scale in many underserved communities. Underdogs are innovating in many sectors and trying to bring their ideas to market every day. In spite of constant failures due to the environment, they keep creating. Once in a while, one of us shines and the world applauds, thinking this is just one exceptional individual when in fact there are millions of us waiting with a breakthrough idea on our laptops but somehow we were born in the wrong family, the wrong community, or the wrong country. Collectively, we can change that, we can unleash innovation at the BOP.

CHAPTER TEN

THE UNDERDOG BERMUDA TRIANGLE

When you're an underdog, you're forced to try things you would never otherwise have attempted.

— MALCOLM GLADWELL

Her dad would make her pitch business solutions in front of the whole family. Born in Montreal, Canada, and moved to the United States at seven, Catherine Hoke grew up with an electrical engineering father who introduced her to innovative thinking and problem-solving. Her dad believed in her, which gives her the confidence to take on the big initiative.

After graduating from the University of California, she worked at Costco selling knives, then worked at Summit Partners, a venture capital firm, which led her to become the Director of Investment Development at American Securities Capital Partners in New York City.

As one of the first female wrestlers on her high school boys' team, Cat experienced the underdog effect earlier in her life. During her tour of the Texas prisons in 2014, after meeting with different felons and able to see the humans behind the orange jumpsuits, she felt empathetic toward the prisoners and reconnected with her underdog soul. That experience shifted everything in Cat's life.

Realizing a lot of felons possessed strong business acumen, sales skills, and entrepreneurial qualities, Catherine developed the Prison Entrepreneurship Program (PEP), a program teaching entrepreneurship and character development to incarcerated men

PEP scaled to more prisons in the state of Texas, graduating around 1,300 students. Compared to the national average of nearly 50 percent, PEP graduates have a three-year recidivism rate of less than 7 percent. As a statement to Cat's leadership and work, in 2017 she received the Texas Governor's Award for Criminal Justice Volunteer Service for Social Innovation, the Manhattan Institute's Social Entrepreneurship Award, and many other prestigious awards. Unfortunately, the fairy tale would turn into a nightmare when Catherine was banned from leading the program by the Texas Department of Criminal Justice because of an affair with a past program participant.

As Catherine put it: *"I became known for a sex scandal instead of all the good work I have poured my life into. So now to be known for this and to get the ejector seat from my own organization. To lose my identity as a passionate young founder and CEO, to lose my identity as a wife. I felt like I had ruined*

God's calling for my life. I had no reason to live anymore. I didn't want to live anymore."

After resigning from PEP, Cat took a year off to reconnect with her soul and do some therapy. While on her soul searching, one day she met an old friend Bill who asked her, "Do you serve people who committed sexual crimes?"

Catherine responded, "The prison system would not let me."

Finally, Bill responded, "What if we created a new program for those people who committed a sexual crime?"

This conversation would inspire Cat to develop Defy Venture in New York City. Its mission is to continue to transform the lives of business leaders and people with criminal histories through their collaboration along the entrepreneurial journey. To this day, Defy has created more than 166 businesses and 350 jobs for graduates.

While Defy continued to gain massive success and rave reviews in the press, a *Daily Beast* article published on March 3, 2018, would crush, once again, the wings of Catherine.[96] She was accused of sexual harassment and other wrongdoing, all investigated by the third-party law firm Wilmer Hale, which found no evidence of wrongdoing. But within a week of these media attacks, she had to resign.

The work started by Cat has been replicated all over the United States, whether through PEP or Defy Venture. Many ex-felons

---

96 (Weill 2018)

have businesses worth hundreds of thousands of dollars. Sometimes in life, you will have to leave the work you started so that it continues to live beyond you. Defy Ventures is what it means to turn the pyramid upside down and empower non-obvious winners. These people were defined by their terrible past, but Defy helped them leverage the potential the world could no longer see in them.

Teddy Moreno, a graduate of Defy Ventures and founder and CEO of Thinkers Thrive, recounts the impact of the program in his life: "Since becoming a member of Defy, I've worked through some demons, and been given the chance to learn about becoming a thriving entrepreneur and shine my own light on those around me. The opportunities presented to me through Defy just keep improving and showing me that anything is possible, regardless of my past."[97]

Defy is rooted in Catherine Hoke's life experience and philosophy of second chances. "I founded Defy as my second chance to give second chances," said Hoke. "I'm the chief operating officer for Defy Ventures, and I work with these people to tell them why second chances are so important."[98]

BREAKING OR MAKING UNDERDOGS
In the old days in Haiti, an oven was three big rocks with firewood in the middle. The rocks kept the pan in balance while the fire cooked the meal. In our lives, the fire is our passion and the pan our motivation. The meal represents our dreams,

---

97 (Teddy n.d.)

98 (Roy 2017)

which need the three rocks to balance them. Motivation and passion aren't enough. The success of an underdog depends on these three rocks: the right environment, resources, and pressure, which I call the "Underdog Bermuda Triangle."

The Bermuda Triangle (or Devil's Triangle)[99] is a region in the western part of the North Atlantic Ocean where aircraft and ships are rumored to have disappeared under strange circumstances. While underdogs have some clear advantages that allow them to survive, succeed, and often thrive, we cannot ignore the unseen forces that are in play at every moment to break the will and crush the vision of any non-obvious winner. No underdog can succeed without a balance of these elements. Besides the personal factors, I can attribute latent innovation and hard life at the BOP to these three elements that are constantly eating our potential leaders, change-makers, and innovators.

Throughout this chapter, I aim to explain how this element can break underdogs or become their lucky break. I will take historical and personal stories to illustrate my arguments.

ENVIRONMENT

I heard this guy talking on the radio about his foundation working to promote entrepreneurship in Haiti. His rise from abject poverty to a financially free life inspired me. As a Haitian, I saw my life in his story.

Days later, I bought his book, then later joined his foundation as a member. This is how I came in contact with Mathias

---

99 (EDITORS 2010)

Pierre, who introduced me to the world of entrepreneurship. Lucky me, I had the opportunity to join him in a "coffee with the boss," where I had the opportunity to sit one-on-one with him in his big office with a wide view of the crowded streets of Delmas. This day, he printed in color a 300-page report about the business opportunities available in Haiti. I could not believe he did it. How could he trust me and give me the tools needed to answer the questions asked? How could he?

I owe what I am doing now to this man and to the environment of hope, excitement, and innovation that was at the Etre Ayisyen Foundation at that time.

James Clear, the renowned writer, stated in his blog post "Motivation is Overvalued. Environment Often Matters More":

"Life is a game and if you want to guarantee better results over a sustained period of time, the best approach is to play the game in an environment that favors you. Winners often win because their environment makes winning easier. That's why successful people hang out with other successful ones. They put themselves in an environment where they can develop their potential and maximize their chance for success."[100]

While I grew up in a difficult neighborhood, I was lucky enough to go to a school that asked a lot of the students. I've seen my grandpa being the voice of reason in his remote village, my uncle organizing the farmers. And the best example of all: my mom spent twenty years teaching at two schools at once. Not all of us underdogs are lucky enough to have

---

100 (Clear n.d.)

people and examples to inspire us and ask us to be the best of us. Therefore, the environment has a great influence on how someone behaves and uses his potential. This is to say: Everyone is a genius. To paraphrase Einstein "*if you judge a fish by its ability to climb a tree, it will live its whole life believing that it is stupid.*"

For an underdog to succeed, the financial, educational, social, and natural environment should be interconnected into a favorable ecosystem that compels underdogs to explore and maximize their unexplored potential; the best human in them.

RESOURCES

Imagine that I am very skilled at alchemy at this current time. My skills in alchemy, although valuable in themselves, aren't suited for the context we are currently living, since chemistry is a better tool for the same issues. We would agree that there's little to no use for my knowledge in these specific circumstances and there are minimal ways I can make an impact with it. This analogy is the same for the BOP. The world cannot expect people at the bottom of the pyramid to go to Paris with a map of Madrid just because both cities are in Europe.

The map used by most people at the BOP is outdated. Their knowledge, skills, and resources are obsolete and won't help them enter this future. Therefore, the lack of access to adequate resources (cutting edge research, books, training, internet, twenty-first-century skills, funding) will propel underdogs forward or destroy them.

In this knowledge economy, we need to know and access information that would increase our likelihood of success. This is what Ayiti Analytics is striving to do in Haiti through data scientist boot camps and meetups. They're exposing our young people to the knowledge needed to build a twenty-first-century world.

There's no need to keep banging our heads on the wrong door. In an environment conducive to personal growth and innovative spirit, our peers can shorten our learning curve by pointing us to the books, tools, and strategies that can help us make better decisions, solve problems, and thrive. It's not really about having resources. It's about having the *right* resources. With the wrong map, you cannot reach your destination, even after 100,000 miles.

PRESSURE

Duality is in almost every corner of life. This is not much different from what we call "stress." Not all stress is bad. In fact, there is positive stress and negative stress. Eustress (from the Greek "eu", meaning good) is a healthy kind of stress that motivates and inspires us to contribute to our community.[101] On the other hand, bad stress triggers depression, anxiety, fatigue, and illness.

Too much negative stress chokes artists, radicalizes human beings, and throws good people into despair. When the pressure becomes unbearable, it crushes your soul and you are stuck in what I call the "Valley of Death," a mental space

---
101 (APA Dictionary of Psychology Search n.d.)

where you resign yourself to your inadequacies, difficulties, and weaknesses as a lifestyle.

Pulitzer Prize-winning author Ernest Becker said one time, "*The artist takes in the world, but instead of being oppressed by it, he reworks it in his own personality and recreates it in the work of art.*" This quotation contains immense truth and wisdom, but I would love to adapt it to the underdogs by saying: The underdog innovator takes in the scarce world he found himself in, but instead of being oppressed by it, he reworks it in his own personality and recreates on a small scale a part of the world he wants to live in. Underdogs have been doing that for years. Some of us get out, but a lot of us are crushed and lost.

We do not have a shortage of pressure at the BOP; on a daily basis, we face pressure to eat, to walk in peace, to shower, to survive, to get transportation, to go to school, and to innovate.

Alleviating some of the burdens to leave us with less stress (because our tolerance for stress is way higher than people living in an environment where life is normal) will unleash a flow of consciousness, creativity, and clarity for all underdogs in the quest to create change and solve problems.

Witnessing the progress of our fellow BOP members produces the eustress (good stress) we need to move toward a more creative life. Nobody wants to be a laggard when everyone else is growing.

We can keep lying to ourselves, but it's harder to lie and disappoint the people who invest and believe in us. If our environment is the car, the pressure is the engine that keeps it moving.

SOCIAL VIBRATION

We vibrate at the frequency of the people around us. I call that "social vibration." To paraphrase author, politician, and social activist Marianne Williamson: *"As we let our own light shine, we unconsciously give others permission to do the same. As we are liberated from our own fear, our presence automatically liberates others."*

The pictures below cement my belief in social vibration. I hope they will do the same for you.

Figure 1. This picture was taken at the Solvay conference in Brussels in 1927. 17 of the scientists in this picture went on to win a Nobel prize.

In Haiti, there are non-confirmed claims among the international and local Christians that in the night of the Ceremony of Bois-Caiman, the story at the beginning of this book, the slaves made a pact with the devil for freedom and that's why Haiti is still struggling. I got a flash of insight while reading.

In many ways, I found this funny, as if their gods wanted them to stay enslaved. I think the magnitude of the accomplishment is difficult to grasp by the human brain.

After reading the book called *Stealing Fire*, I found a scientific explanation for this impossible task accomplished by the slaves: group flow. As they started vibrating on the same level of energy, they got in sync with each other to attain what authors Jamie Wheal and Steven Kotler described as group flow. In this state, words are not even necessary, every entity in the group becomes one.

The same way one person adopts the crowd's attitude during a protest, I predict underserved communities could attain this state when we are feeding off each other's good deeds, actions, and potential. All our energy would converge toward one goal and one goal only: becoming the change we seek to see.

CONCLUSION

We need to create an environment where impossible dreams can be tried. Where resources that can have the highest impact on human lives can be made available, and where we remove the unnecessary stress that eats at the cognitive stamina of BOP innovators'.

The "Underdog Bermuda Triangle" can disintegrate underdogs' potential or it can maximize it, depending on how we organize these three elements.

CHAPTER ELEVEN

UNDERDOGS WHO ARE CHANGING THE WORLD

If you're an underdog, mentally disabled, physically disabled, if you don't fit in, if you're not as pretty as the others, you can still be a hero.
— STEVE GUTTENBERG

While many scholarship programs are based on grades, the Scholarship for Education and Economic Development (SEED) program focuses on candidates with natural leadership skills and those who actively engage their community. SEED is a program developed by Georgetown University and funded by United States Agency for International Development (USAID). It's a two-year program for economically disadvantaged young people from Mexico, Latin America (Honduras, Nicaragua, Salvador), and the Caribbean (the Dominican Republic and Haiti) who are committed to returning to their home country to contribute to its betterment.

Selected students are placed in community colleges around the United States. They spend the first year with a host family, enabling them to improve their English skills and dive into the American culture. They transition into an apartment in the second year, where they live with students from different countries. The whole experience is intended to help students become independent, enhance their leadership ability, equip them with management skills, develop their cross-cultural competencies, and allow them to see themselves as winners.

I was not a good student, so I would have never been able to get any other scholarship if it was not for a program like SEED. It was easy to pick that story to start this chapter because the program is empowering for underdogs. It was the first time in my life I have been in a room where 90 percent of the people had similar stories to mine. Some of them had been abused physically, almost all had come from a very poor background. Some of us came from remote villages and only discovered toilets when we arrived in the US. All of us, and we were all under the age of twenty-five, have been submitted to life's hardest pressures, but we all connected through our shared pain, sorrow, and poverty. To paraphrase the great Ernest Hemingway: *"The world breaks everyone and afterward many are strong at the broken places."*

In SEED, we learned what we were worth through the magic of our unleashed potential. We were getting straight A's, winning contests for our schools, voted for in student government, and volunteering and leading clubs and organizations in a country that was not ours. I was in Wausau, Wisconsin, and we were well-known in the town for our involvement in the community through our volunteer work. Students from the program won professional competitions for Business Professionals of America. We went on to excel at Clinton Global Initiative University, where we competed against people from Yale, Harvard, and so on. Even the mayor of Wausau recognized our power in the community and appointed us all Honorary Citizens. As underdogs, we performed at an elite level; we played in the realm of awesomeness.

Tragically, one year after my graduation, the US State Department shut down the program. Host families all of the country wrote letters to Congress for reconsideration. I was pretty sure I could make something great, but I would not have known what I was capable of if I had not been in the United States. I will always be grateful to the US for giving me that SEED opportunity and this resulting life.

While SEED offered tremendous support, the good life in the United States softened us and reduced our ability to deal with dysfunction in our home country. That's why many students had to go back to the US to get a better life for their family or to continue their schooling. However, I can't find one student who's not attached to their home country or who doesn't have a plan to return to their home and make the difference they set out to make.

On the bright side, dozens of us went on to accomplish what was probably impossible to do in our home country. Equipped with skills, resources, and a strong international network, we are building businesses, writing, running for office, leading change, doing charity work, and impacting the education system in our country. The SEED program shone a bright light on the potential that was hidden in us. And we are just starting. The program did not just empower scholars. It empowered families, communities, and even countries.

The SEED program is the real-life definition of what it means to level the playing field and empower underdogs. It's a confirmation that the ones challenged economically or even the ones who don't have the highest grades, can become winners. A group of non-obvious winners and ignored individuals making moves that would alter the course of many lives. A vivid example of the Underdog Revolution.

Maybe people would say that we were the exception. I don't believe that. We were not, and if you ask any of us, we would tell you that there are many other young people like us in our communities who are better than us. While the BOP is filled with underdogs with potential unexplored, a few of us have exploited our potential and we saw what's possible for us. That's why in this chapter, I want to introduce you to leaders, business people, and community organizers who are now changing the world in a massive way.

HOVARD GUERRIER, HAITI COMPOST BUSINESS, HAITI
"Give me your laptop, your phone, your files, and your ID."

These were the last words the project director told Hovard Guerrier before firing him on a Thursday in October.

No explanation. He had to leave the office on the same day.

Feeling humiliated, with tears in his eyes, Hovard Guerrier left the office with the vision to open the Community Action Plan he developed while studying in the United States.

Born in the touristic village of Labadee in the north part of Haiti, Hovard grew up in an economically-challenged family. His father farmed and fished while his mother sold goods in the streets to be able to provide for him and his siblings. He missed part of his childhood to become a man, fishing with his father and replacing him when he died. A hurricane almost killed him and his father on the sea. His childhood experience made him a man and would later define what he does today. As Hovard says to this day, *"I am not a city boy, I am a farm boy."*

In 2012, Hovard benefited from the Scholarship for Education and Economic Development (SEED), where he majored in Environmental Studies. He wanted to use his skills to improve his community and get a competitive advantage in the Haitian landscape. Being fired from this international organization was Hovard's lucky break. It pushed him to start thinking about the community action plan (CAP) he developed while studying in the United States. The Haiti Composting Business (HCB) produces and sells compost produced from organic waste from residences and business in his hometown in Cap-Haitien.

Hovard started collecting biological waste from neighbors every evening and sorted them. He did not have transportation so he would gather a team with a bucket to go collect waste from several houses and dump them into a land that he borrowed from someone. People started to criticize him because the job was dirty and smelly; his family even tried to convince him to go to the United States after he'd gotten the visa, for which he had been rejected twice.

Hovard never felt that he was less than anyone because his dream is bigger than what most people can see. Three months after he launched, the market validated his concept. He got a contract for 6,000 compost bags. In Haiti, that contract was worth a fortune. From that win, people who did not believe in what he was doing started to support him and got involved more. From that first contract, he bought a tricycle truck and motorcycle that allowed him to collect more waste than he could by hand. As the compost business started flourishing, Hovard saw another opportunity to raise pigs and mix their waste with food waste to continue doing compost. Now HCB is in multiple cities in Haiti, and Hovard is testing new solutions for other problems. Recently, he successfully completed a test using pig manure to create methane. He plans to commercialize this energy solution to fight deforestation and as an alternative to propane.

Hovard is a Clinton Global Initiative University attendee, and his work has been featured in many different media outlets. His vision is to scale to every city through its free franchise mode he used to help other young people also grow. He wants his own HCB site to become a destination for tourists to come and eat fresh vegetables from the farm and for students wanting to learn about environmental sustainability.

As someone who used to sell crafts to tourists, his father used to say, "Every English word is worth one dollar." Today, Hovard is making sure every opportunity counts.

DAQUAN OLIVER, WETHRIVE, UNITED STATES
Born in Mount Vernon, New York, Daquan Oliver witnessed firsthand the tireless dedication of his mother in order to

provide for him and his siblings. He grew distrustful of a system that he witnessed break the hopes and confidence of many of his peers. At fourteen, he made a commitment to become successful and to bring his community with him on his way to success. Olivier's journey is a reflection of this commitment.[102]

During his bachelor's degree in Business Management from Babson College, Daquan founded *WeThrive* as a way to provide a holistic set of skills to vulnerable young middle and high schoolers like he once was. Through the program, students learn life skills, start real companies and social movements, and also earn money. WeThrive operates in Los Angeles, Oakland, San Francisco, San Jose, East Palo Alto, Washington, DC, and New York City.[103]

The program is "very tech-enabled," said Oliver. Quality control is ensured by a web and mobile app that collects data from teachers and students.

The WeThrive site says, "Youth participants learn life skills such as goal setting, public speaking (which builds confidence), and personal finance. They practice these skills each session until they become a habit. Ultimately, we use business creation solely as a vehicle to prepare our students to accomplish their goals and navigate a path of opportunity."[104]

Since we met at the Clinton Global Initiative University in 2016, Daquan has been featured on the 2017 *Forbes*'s "30 Under

---

102 (Let's Give A Damn Podcast 2018)
103 (Goode 2018)
104 (WeThrive n.d.)

30 List," *The Boston Globe*, "Boston's 25 Under 25," and delivered a TEDx Talk.

Starting such a program is personal for Daquan. As many underdogs, instead of using his pain to withdraw from the world, he uses it to prevent others from going through a similar situation and widen their horizon, as he said:

"As a child of low-income background, I relate to and understand not only the very issues our youth participants face but also some of the steps forward to succeed despite those issues. Working together with schools, community-based organizations, college students, advisors, and mentors."[105]

NZINGAH ONIWOSAN, YES BABY I LIKE IT RAW, UNITED STATES-HAITI

"*I want to learn Chinese medicine,*" Nzingah always said when she was just a kid. In 1992, when she was eleven, after breaking up a violent fight between her mom and her mom's husband, she realized that her mother was hurt and that her mother would never be the same. Nzingah said, "My mother died that day." Nzingah grew up with a mother suffering from manic depression, now called bipolar disorder; she never got to experience the mother-daughter bond that she, fortunately, was able to build with her grandmother instead.

As if her pain was not enough, nature would submit her to molestation and abuse from the same man. She would often lock herself in her room and sleep with a knife in case this

---

105 (WeThrive n.d.)

man came to touch her. He manipulated her, telling if she ever said something, her mother would get worse. An unbearable pain for a young girl, Nzingah was also afraid to be taken away to the foster care system. Art was the venue where Nzingah would express her struggles, under the supervision of an art teacher who saw her creative soul and gave it life. *"Art saved my life,"* said Nzingah, *"because I could've killed him, but I never went there."*

While her mother's situation was getting worse and she was acting like a crazy person, Nzingah became physically sick. At nineteen, she had five physicians seeing her on a regular basis because of a prolactinoma (pituitary tumor) and scleroderma (an autoimmune disorder). *"I was sick and tired of being sick and tired,"* recalled Nzingah. That's when she started doing more research on healthy living and veganism and decided to take her health into her own hands.

"I made the changes and weaned myself off the drugs. I became a certified holistic health consultant, raw vegan chef, and yoga instructor so I could own my healing process. My autoimmune disorder is now in remission and the major side effects of my prolactinoma (irregular and heavy menstrual cycle) has been eliminated."[106]

Since these changes, Nzingah has been healthier than ever, and while trying to heal herself, she also became a healer for others. Nzingah's philosophy is simple: *"Become the you you wanted for others."* She has dedicated her life to teaching kids with disabilities by leveraging art. Her company *Yes Baby I*

---

106 (blackvegansrock.com/ n.d.)

Like It Raw promotes healthy living and helps people become their healthiest version through food, lifestyle, and art. She is actively working on democratizing yoga by bringing it to the streets of Haiti.

Nzingah's work has been featured at several museums and galleries, such as Cornel Museum in Delray Beach, Old Dillard Museum in Fort Lauderdale, and Amadlozi Gallery in Miami. She also appeared in Creative Mornings and the 100 Years of Beauty campaign produced by Cut, a Seattle storytelling company.

During the rough time, Nzingah always tells herself, "*His mercy shall endure.*" She believes we can all become what we are not, yet. She plans to continue her neuroscience degree and open a health and trauma center. Instead of letting her pain destroy her sense of self and withdraw from the world, Nzingah uses it to transform the lives of physically challenged and health-challenged underdogs.

BRUNELLO CUCINELLI, BRUNELLO CUCINELLI, ITALY

Born into a peasant family in the village of Castel Rigone near Perugia, Brunello Cucinelli soon noticed the way he used to be looked down upon while wearing peasant clothing. The humiliation in his father's eyes every time he came home from his back-breaking job at the cement factory compelled the young Brunello to bring something valuable to the world and treat people with humanity.

In 1978, after dropping out of his engineering degree, Brunello got a $500 loan to start a new trend of dyed cashmere. After marrying Frederica Benda, he moved to the town of Solomeo in 1982, where he would build his new empire and work of art, the Brunello Cuccinelli luxury brand, around cashmere clothing.

The brand focuses on handcrafted attention to detail and creativity and is built around the Humanistic Enterprise model revolving on Italian craftsmanship, sustainable growth, and exclusive positioning and distribution. Located in an old castle surrounded by medieval houses, the company made more than $6 million in 2017 and the Brunello network is worth $1.6 billion in 2020.[107] But what's special about Brunello? Why include him here?

Brunello did not just build his factory in Solomeo—he renovated the small town. He helped renovate the village churches, like the Church of St. Bartholomew. He also built a beautiful 250-seat theater, repaved streets, built a small library, and built public squares and a woodland park. When Brunello speaks, he quotes the great philosophers and poets who have graced our world with their ingenuity. He's not your typical businessman; he's more of an artist. His father played a huge role in the humanistic way he builds his business. Every time Brunello would achieve any financial or social success, he recalled his father saying to always stay a good man.

Besides donating 20 percent of the company profit, Brunello pays his workers higher than the market rate and forbids employees to work past 5 p.m. because he says that "stifles the muse" and destroys the mind-soul-work balance. There are

---

107 (CUOFANO n.d.)

ninety-minute breaks where employees can go home or pay less than €3 to enjoy a copious lunch where Pellegrino and wine, minestre, pastas, platters of grilled meat, and salad are served. Brunello is a Renaissance man. Silicon Valley execs are flocking to his house to listen to him speak and learn how to develop a more humanistic company. Brunello puts human dignity at the center of his business, as evident when he poetically says:

"In my organization, the focal point is the common good, which is the guiding force in pursuing prudent and courageous actions. In my business, people are at the very center of every production process because I am convinced that human dignity is restored solely through the rediscovery of the conscience. Work elevates human dignity and the emotional ties that derive from it."

Brunello also thinks about the next generation and will continue to pass the value of craftsmanship through his Solomeo's School of Arts and Crafts established in 2013, an important element of the humanistic enterprise model.

"In the humanistic enterprise of Solomeo, we work and pursue the same objective, but above all, we comply with a system of non-material beliefs that we all acknowledge as part of our entire company. I would not like to live in a world where everything boils down to mere profit. Money is valuable only when it is spent to improve man's life and growth, and this is the end that I struggle to achieve."

Brunello received many great accolades all over the world. He was named "Cavaliere del Lavoro" (Knight of Industry) by the president of Italy and received an honorary degree in Philosophy and Ethics of Human Relations by the University of Perugia. [108]

LOUINO ROBILLARD, KONBIT BIBLIYOTÈK, CITÉ SOLEIL

"Konbit (meaning solidarity) is the soul of Haiti. Every culture has its soul and the concept is what connects us together," said Louino Robillard, one of the key figures behind the library project in Cité Soleil.

Raised in Cité Soleil, Louino Robillard earned a Master's in Applied Community Change and Peace Building. He wrote a research paper on the traditional form of cooperation in Haiti called "Konbit," a concept he has been applying in many local projects in Haiti, especially in his own neighborhood, Cité Soleil, known for gang violence and inhuman poverty.

When Louino announced to his wife that he was resigning from his well-paid job at an international organization, she asked him for his plan, which he did not have. He simply knew that he had to pour his soul into restoring dignity and hope in Cité Soleil. Louino believes it's up to his neighborhood to create something for Haiti and the world because they are always being handed help. The library is not just the goal, Louino wants the world to witness the potential not yet explored in the young people in Cité Soleil, getting rid of ignorance to make a place for innovation.

---

108 (CUOFANO n.d., Mead 2010)

The model of Konbit is based on five pillars:

1. participation,

2. collaboration,

3. interdependence,

4. transparency, and

5. human energy.

Participation and collaboration are important. Haiti has used and borrowed models from all over the world. Louino thinks this is our last strategy, utilizing our own model, the model on which the country's independence is built.

In 2014, he launched the Cité Soleil Peace Prize, an annual initiative that honors ordinary young people who are making an extraordinary impact in their neighborhoods in Cité Soleil. When asked for the reason behind the Initiative, Louino stated: *"I want the world to recognize the potential in our community, and I want our young people to recognize the potential in themselves."*

For Louino, this project serves as moral debt that Cité Soleil owes Haiti. Today the project has already been supported by a very diverse group of 6,000 donors who have donated $216,800 and 21,807 books. We can witness the tremendous impact of Louino's concept of Konbit through Konbit Bilbiyotèk Solèy, which is a community-owned, led, and funded library happening in Cité Soleil. Once called the most gang-affected area in Haiti, this community is now building the largest library in Haiti.

GERARD ADAMS, FOWNDERS, NEW JERSEY

The red and blue lights flashed across his eyes before he was arrested for selling drugs. Gerard Adams was born in 1984 in New Jersey, and early in life, he learned trading from his father and became a millionaire by twenty-four. On top of the world, he lost it all.[109]

As a former drop-out of Caldwell University and with little formal education, Gerard was lost. Looking for a way out, Gerard and his intern started Elite Daily, a media company for millennials. Elite Daily grew to 41 million readers, and $400,000 in revenue, each month.[110] Following this success, Gerard was listed by *Business Insider* among the top "100 Most Influential People in Silicon Valley."

As Gerard believes, *"Our background doesn't matter as much as our desire. I believe wholeheartedly that with the right focus and consistency, anyone can live this life."* After taking time off, Gerard decided to go back to his community in New Jersey to launch *Fownders*.[111]

Fownders is Gerard's commitment to empower minority communities and give back to his own community. With 20,000-square-feet of workspace and eighteen apartments where entrepreneurs are connected to mentors, resources, and a community to launch their entrepreneurial journey in Newark, New Jersey, Fownders is a social impact accelerator dedicated to creating a community for young entrepreneurs.

---

109 (Bilyeu 2017)
110 (Shontell 2014)
111 (About Gerard n.d.)

The building was in a deserted area that Gerard wanted to revive through entrepreneurship. Contrary to city development that forces people out of the city being renovated, the development manager believes "*When redevelopment happens, the goal should be to integrate the existing community, not push them out. It's why we are considering the case of Fownders as part of our ongoing study of organizations and people who are shifting innovation. Who place the community at the core of their innovation.*"[112]

CONCLUSION

This book could just be a book only about stories of underdogs. These few mini-stories are among dozens of stories I had to pick from to prove that the many constraints faced by underdogs are exactly what pushes them to create the rewarding world so many of them are now creating.

I have met many of the people presented in this chapter and I would vouch for their work and the kind of inspiration they bring to me and to their respective communities. They are the light that brightens the imagination of people at the bottom of the pyramid. They are the hope and dreams of many who wish to make a dent in the universe.

In spite of all of the challenges and an unlevel playing field, they have managed to make an impact. While some of them have had the support they needed, others do not. So I encourage you to reach out if you can. Support in different ways. Because when those people's dreams die, they do not die alone. They take with them an entire generation's dreams.

---

112 (Hunckler 2017, Fry 2017)

CHAPTER TWELVE

APPLYING UNDERDOG INNOVATION

The reasonable man adapts himself to the world: the unreasonable one persists in trying to adapt the world to himself. Therefore all progress depends on the unreasonable man.

— GEORGE BERNARD SHAW

One individual without formal education and an engineering degree turned a fifty-mile journey into a five-mile road with his bare hands and a few rudimentary tools. Armed with will and a vision of the world that others did not see, he created a brand-new world for his community and became an inspiration for generations to come.

Dashrath Manjhi was an Indian laborer who lived in a small village called Gehlaur in India. With only two goats under his name, he lived with his wife whom he loved unconditionally. Dashrath would become a legend in the history of India because of his will, persistence, and creating the future without the proper tools.

The town of Gehlaur was disconnected from the next town because of a steep and rocky mountain that would take fifty miles for the inhabitants to travel around.

In 1959, while carrying his lunch to him working on the other side of the mountain, his wife fell and died the same year because of the impossible and deadly crusade through the mountain to get to the nearest hospital. Dashrath's world turned upside down, losing his companion, his friend, the woman he loved more than anything.

As it came to Viktor Frankl, the author of *Man's Search for Meaning,* while in the Nazi's concentration camp, *"Everything can be taken from a man but one thing: the last of the human freedoms—to choose one's attitude in any given set of circumstances. To choose one's way."*[113] Manjhi decided to dedicate his whole life to a grander mission. He quit his farming job, sold his goats, and went to the top of the mountain. Every day for the next twenty-two years, he would chisel the giant mountain little by little. People laughed at him and called him crazy, but he continued even after hurting himself multiple times. The government even arrested him because it was illegal to damage a mountain in India, but he persisted.

From his twenty-two years of relentless work, he carved a road thirty feet deep, thirty feet wide, and 360 feet long. He turned a painful and rocky journey of fifty miles into five miles, allowing students to attend school and villagers to access the nearest town to manage their daily lives. The

---

113 (Frankl 1946)

government honored him after this achievement and gave him some land, which he donated for a new hospital. He advocated for the government to tar the road, but they only did thirty years later – when it had only taken twenty-two years to dig it.

To date, he's considered "The Man Who Moved a Mountain." [114]

All over the world at the BOP, people are dying with dreams in mind and innovation and creation that the world may never see. The cycle continues decade after decade. For some of us lucky ones, we will probably make an impact and the world will talk about us and applaud us like we are something special, cut from specific cloth. In fact, I *know* there are more like us than the world can imagine. Because when I see them, I see myself in them. As an underdog myself, we recognize the potential in each other. That is why I write this book, to let the world know there are more of us. I am not pretending that I hold all the solutions and that there are no other models to create innovation and face poverty, but I am 100 percent confident that the only way to create a strong and independent BOP is by turning the pyramid upside down and empowering the non-obvious winners. How many of us will continue to die without ever seeing the change we seek to make? How many?

As much I want people supporting my vision for the world, this is not a plea for myself, so look in your own community, church, and life to find the non-obvious winner you can

---

114 (Josceline Anne Mascarenhas 2018, Ventures 2015)

empower. Because they are everywhere. In the slums in India as well as in many neighborhoods in the richest countries in the world.

Applying underdog innovation model should not be solely for the social development sector or for underserved communities. It can become a way of thinking, managing, and leading in every sector of life. We need different actors to play their respective roles in identifying, rewarding, and scaling ideas, businesses, way of life, and successes that are already working at the BOP. To accomplish such heroic work, we will need to consider all the following sectors.

PRIVATE ENTERPRISE
Private enterprise can apply this method in their hiring process by identifying some rejected applications that might have the potential, but they pass because of their "obvious winner" bias. They can also involve their different departments in crafting a work culture or bringing new services or products into the market. They can develop new and innovative payment models to allow underserved communities to purchase what they are selling. Instead of simply donating items, large corporations can co-create with BOP innovators products that can change lives as well as make them a profit. Making an impact doesn't mean you cannot make a profit. TOMS Shoes is one of the best examples in our time of this. Corporations' success metrics should include the bottom line as well as social impact.

When enterprises do incorporate social responsibility or sponsoring, they should also consider sponsoring organizations that are not the most popular, or events that have an impact on the way people live and think.

CIVIL SOCIETY

To successfully empower the BOP, civil society should not be just civil, it should be active. That's why leaders in the BOP should try to engage the civil society where they spend most of their time—public markets, churches, public transportations, etc. Instead of asking them to come to us, underdog leaders need to go to them to engage them in co-creating the world we seek to build. Hovard Guerrier is a social entrepreneur solving the trash issues in the northern part of Haiti. He would never have been one had he not involved his community in the project.

Finally, organizing events that highlight good behavior displayed by vulnerable groups would invite other groups to do the same. Radio stations can create programs for rewarding normal citizens for their good behavior and educate them on how to build the community we seek to build. I dream of a radio station that only highlights the good work, daily good deeds, and acts of kindness of the people. As Gary "Garyvee" Vaynerchuk likes to say, *"Let's make positivity louder."*

LOCAL ORGANIZATIONS

Create local organizations that allow people at the BOP to access needed services like lawyers, doctors, engineers, designers, architects and so on. For instance, if someone at the BOP wants to run for office, unless they have a good connection, they likely won't get the resources they need. But if they get credit to access lawyers or designers, they have a better chance to run and win. In Haiti, a lot of entrepreneurs have a problem with creating a financial plan or playing with their numbers. But they could get credit or support for accessing these services through local specialized organizations. Of course, this would give them a competitive advantage and perhaps allow them to go to a bank and find themselves eligible for a loan.

LOCAL GOVERNMENT

Ghettos won't produce symphonies and create technological innovation when you feed them guns or if their environment allows the worst in them to flourish. I visited Lawndale, Chicago, five years ago and met many talented students who think their fate is sealed and nothing can be done to achieve positive change. The current environment in underserved communities has produced people who are willing—even eager—to create the bad rather than the good.

Creating an environment that helps underdogs to flourish is the sacred work of any government that respects itself. Therefore the government should remove bottlenecks and remove the unnecessary barriers that only prevent those without resources to access a certain level. Government programs and laws should take into consideration the lowest of us if they want the lowest of us to progress. That progression will result in more of us paying taxes and supporting life in the community.

BOP CONSUMERS

Consumer think tanks can be created where any individual can submit ideas or innovative ways to change things to consider, vote on, then share with the larger public. When BOP consumers find bad products, there is rarely any way they can report bad corporate behavior. Consumer protection groups need to be created to represent the needs of these people and make their voices heard. One of the common problems at the BOP is the dehumanization of each other. Because we have not been treated as a human should be treated, we think it's okay to pursue this behavior in our respective community and social circles. Public transportation and food quality should be assessed to ensure human health and dignity. People at the BOP should be encouraged to create a standard of living for their respective community and ensure that they see each other as human beings, demanding the absolute best from each other. We will not be able to thrive if we don't treat each other as fellow humans.

It's sad to say this here, but I have been discriminated against more by my own people in my own country than when I was living in the whitest of places such as Wausau, Wisconsin. The scarcity of dignity made it an excuse for bad corporate behavior and terrible customer service.

BOP ENTREPRENEURS
Entrepreneurs at the BOP should start organizing themselves in groups to lobby through the congress of their community and push legislators to vote laws and government programs that facilitate business creation, investment, and scaling. The BOP can also look for buying-in of their respective communities through pre-sales and petitions to ensure what they are bringing to market is validated and so banks and investors can see the value in it for them.

Social entrepreneurs can focus on creating programs that are more skills- and resources-oriented and use a charity component as an add-on to the main purpose.

Social entrepreneurs must leverage technology to create knowledge hubs where they can share practices, successes, and failures in order to educate the ones who are farther away in their social entrepreneur journey, making sure transformational information is evenly distributed and not skewed to a few lucky ones in the cities. Learning from each other and working together to solve the same problem in our respective communities requires less energy and might be innovative because it takes into account the culture and view of diverse communities.

DEVELOPMENT AND AID AGENCIES

Development agencies and aid agencies often have the most readily available resources in all these categories and want to demonstrate results at least as good as their past results, despite what might be mistrust between communities and them. They will need to think about new ways of developing, creating, and funding projects to include the broader community, not just the (few at the top) stakeholders and real decision-makers. They will need to work with social entrepreneurs and local governments to help them come up with a project. A lot of times, big aid agencies have their area of focus and they force local people to create something in that area of focus even when the particular kind of help is not needed.

Development aid agencies can create and fund radio stations with the purpose of educating people and helping them adhere to movements that create the betterment of their community.

They can also fund "local specialized organizations" to help them provide services to people at the BOP who would not otherwise be able to access these good quality services, which boosts these sectors and also help the BOP at the same time. For instance, fund a lawyer association to provide low-cost law services, or a branding company that could provide low-cost services for entrepreneurs who have good products but weak branding.

They can work with a local bank to provide a loan at good rates for innovative ideas. Because of their global presence and reach, they could also work with large corporations like Facebook, Amazon, Twitter, and PayPal to open their respective platforms to the BOP. So maybe instead of Amazon building wells in Africa, they could invest in some sellable local products and make them available online.

SCHOOLS
The education system focuses on creating think-alike individuals. Instead of encouraging students to become creative, it stifles their creativity. A school must not only focus on the standard learning curriculum but also create a space for students to explore their potential and talents. As Sir Kenneth Robinson beautifully said in his now-famous TED Talk entitled *Do Schools Kill Creativity?* "Many highly talented, brilliant, creative people think they're not—because the thing they were good at school wasn't valued, or was actually stigmatized."[115]

---

115 (Robinson 2016)

When students grow up in an underserved community, we must equip them with the soft skills and space to create and think creatively. Entrepreneurial clubs, product creation camps, field trips, design thinking, and creativity labs should be an inherent part of the learning process. Even if each school cannot have one, at least we could have one in each city.

Access to information should be proportional to rich schools as well as poor schools. If the BOP cannot access great teachers because of purchasing power, the government should ensure they can access the same level of information through tech solutions, mobile learning centers (buses for mobile internet or lab), and community resource centers. Enrollment and grading (if there's grading at all) should focus not just on the ones with the highest IQ and grades, but on students' ability to think creatively, solve problems, and become a better human being. What's the point of getting the best grades if they strip away our ability to solve the problems our fellow humans face or better the world we live in? We need to grade for hard skills and also for soft skills, and we need to learn how to measure both better.

CONCLUSION

Without a concerted effort of the different sectors, inequality will continue to rise and the BOP will continue to be a burden for the rich countries, a testing lab for researchers, and a place for some people to experience poverty. My recommendations aren't perfect. So I am inviting you to submit your ideas or things that you have done in the community that are working so we all over the world can learn from other resilient communities, groups, and individuals.

Inequality is not caused by rich people; inequality is enabled by a system that allows people at the top of every sphere to decide how people at the bottom should live their lives. It's not just money issues, it's also a power imbalance where if you are helping me you want to decide *how* to help me instead of figuring out my real needs. Billionaires can continue to invest millions of dollars in Africa, but until the underdogs in Africa are also empowered to work on the problems, voice their view, and participate actively in the change, it will be a lot of effort without much return. We can build infrastructure, but it will crumble if you don't build human capital to manage them and understand their value.

The underdog approach can be applied in every sector, every situation, and every organization. The principles are simple, but those principles demand we be unreasonable: to imagine and create a world where every potential can be explored. At least if we fall short, we are falling short of creating a greater world.

CONCLUSION

MY IDEALISTIC VIEW OF THE FUTURE

"Our deepest fear is not that we are inadequate. Our deepest fear is that we are powerful beyond measure. It is our light, not our darkness that most frightens us. We ask ourselves, 'Who am I to be brilliant, gorgeous, talented, and fabulous?' Actually, who are you not to be? You are a child of God. Your playing small does not serve the world. There is nothing enlightened about shrinking so that other people will not feel insecure around you. We are all meant to shine as children do. We were born to make manifest the glory of God that is within us. It is not just in some of us; it is in everyone and as we let our own light shine, we unconsciously give others permission to do the same. As we are liberated from our own fear, our presence automatically liberates others."
— MARIANNE WILLIAMSON

Our evil is a mask, a mask we wear to hide our goodness. It's so easy for us to believe the end of the world is near but difficult to grasp the idea that the renewal of the world is near. I believe in our ability to create this idealistic world that our kids daydream about. We've cured diseases, gone to the moon, invented artificial intelligence; we are well able to reduce human-enable suffering in this world.

I have included a number of facts in this book to make sure it was scientifically sound and based on real data. Above all, I have one specific goal in writing this conclusion: Leaping from facts to faith.

Martin Luther King's dreams were not rooted in science but in faith. Even going to the moon was not rooted in science at first; it started with a dream. The Underdog Revolution will not be rooted just in science but in human potential and dignity. As we become more educated and informed, the more our realistic view paints a darker future. Our current circumstance and logical minds can't foresee the future we must reorganize for our children. Therefore, we must also rely on our hearts and faith.

The current state of the world might prevent us from dreaming or even believing in a new world. Believe me, for every twenty terrible things you hear in the news, there are thousands of good actions that we don't hear about. It's possible that we might never reach this utopian world, but at least we are striving for the very best instead of settling for what it is.

The dreamers, leaders, and shakers of our time aren't better than any of us. Their world-changing ideas and actions don't stem from a lack of internal darkness, they have lit their light so much that it shattered their darkness, making us only see the light. What if we all strive to brighten our light, for ourselves and for our community?

I believe your belief in a greater world is essential to the process.

I am confident we can all take bold actions that get us closer to our idealistic world.

I have trust in your human instinct.

I have trust in your humanity to acknowledge the humanity in everyone you meet.

Let's strive for the unthinkable.

APPENDIX

INTRODUCTION

Vulliamy, Ed. 2015. August 2015. Accessed 2019. https://www.theguardian.com/culture/2015/aug/28/10-best-revolutionaries-che-guevara-mahatma-gandhi-leon-trotsky.

Kaisary, Philip James. 2008 . *The Literary Impact of The Haitian Revolution* . March .

CHAPTER 1

Talamas, Dr Sean. 2016. *Smart at first sight.* July 4.

Manko, Marni. 2013. *The Weird and Wonderful World According to Seth Godin.* November 1. Accessed 2019. https://monetate.com/blog/the-weird-and-wonderful-world-according-to-seth-godin/.

17, 1 Samuel. n.d. *Bible, New International Version.*

Gupta, Soham. 2014. "What is the origin of the word underdog." *timesofindia. indiatimes.com.* July 17. Accessed 2019. https://timesofindia.indiatimes.com/What-is-the-origin-of-the-word-underdog/articleshow/782032.cms.

Barber, Nicholas. 2016. "Is Rocky 'the most successful bad film ever made'?" *BBC.* November 9. Accessed 2019. http://www.bbc.com/culture/story/20161109-is-rocky-the-most-successful-bad-film-ever-made?ocid=fbcul.

ELLER, CLAUDIA. 2019. *Variety Magazine.* July. Accessed 2019. https://variety.com/2019/film/features/sylvester-stallone-rocky-ownership-stake-1203275639/.

Study.com. n.d. *Social Categorization: Theory and Definition Chapter 8 / Lesson 15 Transcript.* Accessed 2019. https://study.com/academy/lesson/social-categorization-theory-and-definition.html.

Psychology Today. n.d. *Social Comparison Theory*. Accessed 2019.
https://www.psychologytoday.com/intl/basics/social-comparison-theory.

McLeod, Saul. 2019. *Social Identity Theory*. Accessed 2019.
https://www.simplypsychology.org/social-identity-theory.html.

Posten, Merritt. 1998. *Living in a Social World*. Accessed 2019.
https://www.units.miamioh.edu/psybersite/fans/bc.shtml.

Goldschmied, Nadav. 2005. *The underdog effect: Definition, limitations, and motivations. why do we support those at a competitive disadvantage?* University of South Florida, July 19.

Study.com. n.d. *Distributive Justice: Definition, Theory, Principles & Examples*. Accessed 2019.
https://study.com/academy/lesson/distributive-justice-definition-theory-principles-examples.html.

Ellemers, Naomi. n.d. *Social identity theory*. Accessed 2019.
https://www.britannica.com/topic/social-identity-theory.

POPOVA, MARIA. 2014. *Fixed vs. Growth: The Two Basic Mindsets That Shape Our Lives*. January 29. Accessed 2019.
https://www.brainpickings.org/2014/01/29/carol-dweck-mindset/.

University of California Television (UCTV). 2018. *New Skills and Brain Plasticity*. Youtube Video.

Gaines, Cork. 2019. *Tom Brady was the biggest steal in NFL Draft history, but there was more to it than just luck*. February 3. Accessed 2019.
https://www.businessinsider.sg/patriots-draft-tom-brady-2017-1/.

CHAPTER 2

United Nations. n.d. *Goal 1: End poverty in all its forms everywhere*. Accessed 2019.
https://www.un.org/sustainabledevelopment/poverty/.

Malik, Khalid. 2014. *Sustaining Human Progress: Reducing Vulnerabilities and Building Resilience*. United Nations Development Programme, United Nations Development Programme, 19.

Elks, Sonia. 2018. *Global goal to end poverty by 2030 unlikely to be met, World Bank says*. Reuters. September 19. Accessed 2019.
https://www.reuters.com/article/us-global-development-poverty/global-goal-to-end-poverty-by-2030-unlikely-to-be-met-world-bank-says-idUSKCN1LZ2JL.

World Population Review . n.d. "World Population Review ." *Population of Cities in Haiti (2020)*. Accessed 2019.
http://worldpopulationreview.com/countries/haiti-population/cities/.

Analysys Mason. 2019. "KNOWLEDGE CENTRE MOBILE SERVICES IN SUB-SAHARAN AFRICA: TRENDS AND FORECASTS 2019–2024FOLLOW US KNOWLEDGE CENTRE 0 0Google +0EmailPrint Mobile services in Sub-Saharan Africa: trends and forecasts 2019–2024."
https://www.analysysmason.com/. August 2. Accessed 2020. https://www.analysysmason.com/Research/Content/Regional-forecasts-/Mobile-services-SSA-RDMM0/.

GSMA. 2018. "More Than Half of Sub-Saharan Africa to be Connected to Mobile by 2025, Finds New GSMA Study." *gsma.com*. Uly 17. Accessed 2019. https://www.gsma.com/newsroom/press-release/more-than-half-of-sub-saharan-africa-to-be-connected-to-mobile-by-2025-finds-new-gsma-study/.

Belinda Baah, Nika Naghavi. 2018. "How smartphones will drive future opportunities for the mobile money industry." GSMA, London , 4.

Knoema. n.d. *Haiti - Share of the Internet users*. Accessed 2020. https://knoema.com/atlas/Haiti/Share-of-the-Internet-users.

Treanor, Morag. 2017. "Dispelling the Myth of Parental 'Poverty of Aspiration': Morag Treanor and the Impact of Poverty on Children and Young People." *connect. scot*. December. Accessed 2019. https://connect.scot/teacher-professional/resources/dispelling-myth-parental-poverty-aspiration-morag-treanor.

Robert Muggah, Katie Hill. 2018. *African cities will double in population by 2050. Here are 4 ways to make sure they thrive*. June 27. Accessed 2019. https://www.weforum.org/agenda/2018/06/Africa-urbanization-cities-double-population-2050-4%20ways-thrive/.

World Economic Forum. 2019. "Time required to start a business (days)." *Doing Business*. Accessed 2019. https://data.worldbank.org/indicator/IC.REG.DURS.

2019. "The Prosperity Paradox,." In *How Innovation Can Lift Nations Out of Poverty*, by Efosa Ojomo, Karen Dillon Clayton Christensen, Audiobook. Harper Business .

Ong'ayo, Antony Otieno. 2008. *Political instability in Africa Where the problem lies and alternative perspectives*. Wageningen, September 19.

Norris McDonald, Jamaica Gleaner. 2019. *Haiti's Huge Gold Reserve: 'Haiti, Give Me Your Gold, Not Your Weak and Weary!'.* April 21st. Accessed September 2019. https://www.globalresearch.ca/haitis-huge-gold-reserve-haiti-give-me-your-gold-not-your-weak-and-weary/5675490.

EFFICA-GROUP. n.d. *AFRICA-THE EMERGING CONTINENT*. Accessed 2019. http://effica-group.com/africa.

IGHOBOR, KINGSLEY. 2013. *Africa's youth: a "ticking time bomb" or an opportunity?* May. Accessed 2019. https://www.un.org/africarenewal/magazine/may-2013/africa%E2%80%99s-youth-%E2%80%9Cticking-time-bomb%E2%80%9D-or-opportunity.

Central Intelligence Agency. n.d. *CENTRAL AMERICA :: HAITI*. Accessed 2019. https://www.cia.gov/library/publications/the-world-factbook/geos/ha.html.

Tran, Mark. 2012. *Are natural resources a blessing or a curse for developing countries?* The Guardian. October 25. Accessed 2019. https://www.theguardian.com/global-development/2012/oct/25/natural-resources-blessing-curse-developing-countries.

CHAPTER 3

Prabhu, Jaideep. 2012. "Jugaad Innovation." In *Think Frugal, Be Flexible, Generate Breakthrough Growth*, by Simone Ahuja Navi Radjou, 9-13. Jossey-Bass.

Gladwell, Malcom. 2017. "FOOD FIGHT." *Revisionisthistory Podcast.*

CBS. 2010. *Haiti Gets a Penny of Each U.S. Aid Dollar.* January 27. Accessed 2019. https://www.cbsnews.com/news/haiti-gets-a-penny-of-each-us-aid-dollar/.

World Bank. n.d. *The developing world's 4.5 billion low-income people already a $5 trillion market.* Accessed 2019.
http://datatopics.worldbank.org/consumption/market.

Statista. 19. *Number of mobile cellular subscriptions per 100 inhabitants in Haiti from 2000 to 2018.* July. Accessed 2020.
https://www.statista.com/statistics/502111/mobile-cellular-subscriptions-per-100-inhabitants-in-haiti/.

González, Ángel. 2015. *Push to make Haiti an e-cash economy fell far short.* Accessed 2019.
https://special.seattletimes.com/o/flatpages/nationworld/haiti-shaky-recovery-part-2-earthquake-five-years-later-annivers.html.

Reficco, Ezequiel. 2016. *6 reasons companies fail to reach the bottom of the pyramid.* 16 April. Accessed 2019.
https://www.devex.com/news/6-reasons-companies-fail-to-reach-the-bottom-of-the-pyramid-80719.

CHAPTER 4

Stillman, Jessica. 2016. Inc Magazine. April 26. Accessed 2019.
https://www.inc.com/jessica-stillman/9-definitions-of-creativity-to-inspire-you.html.

Rosso, Brent D. 2014. *Creativity and Constraints: Exploring the Role of Constraints in the Creative Processes of Research and Development Teams.* Missoula, Marc. Creativity and Constraints: Exploring the Role of Constraints in the Creative Processes of Research and Development Teams.

Neren, Uri. 2011. *The Number One Key to Innovation: Scarcity.* January 14. Accessed 2019. https://hbr.org/2011/01/the-number-one-key-to-innovati.

CICIORA, PHIL. 2015. *Scarcity, not abundance, enhances consumer creativity, study says.* University Of Illinois. November 16. Accessed 2019.
https://news.illinois.edu/view/6367/279507.

SONENSHEIN, SCOTT. 2017. *How Constraints Force Your Brain To Be More Creative.* July 2. Accessed 2019.
https://www.fastcompany.com/3067925/how-constraints-force-your-brain-to-be-more-creative.

Lienhard, John H. n.d. *WRIGHT AND LANGLEY.* Accessed 2019.
https://uh.edu/engines/epi32.htm.

Barry Jaruzelski, Robert Chwalik, and Brad Goehle. 2018. "WHAT THE TOP INNOVATORS GET RIGHT." *Strategy + Business*, October 30.

CHAPTER 5

'Utoikamanu, Fekitamoeloa. n.d. *Closing the Technology Gap in Least Developed Countries*. Accessed 2020.
https://www.un.org/en/chronicle/article/closing-technology-gap-least-developed-countries.

CHAPTER 6

Food and Agriculture Organization of the United Nations. 2019. "The State Of Food Security & Nutrition In The World." *http://www.fao.org/*. Accessed 220.
http://www.fao.org/3/ca5162en/ca5162en.pdf.

Mendoza-Salonga, Prof. Aida. 2104. *Nutrition and brain development*. August 15.

Stewart, Frances. 2002. *Root causes of violent conflict in developing countriesCommentary: Conflict—from causes to prevention?* February 9.

World Bank. 2017. *The Global Findex Database 2017*. Accessed 2019.
https://globalfindex.worldbank.org/basic-page-overview.

Bogmans, Christian. 2019. *Falling Costs Make Wind, Solar More Affordable*. April 26. Accessed 2019.
https://blogs.imf.org/2019/04/26/falling-costs-make-wind-solar-more-affordable/.

Nichols, Greg. 2016. *Promising trend for innovators: 3D printer prices are falling*. Feb 4. Accessed 2019.
https://www.zdnet.com/article/promising-trend-for-innovators-3d-printer-prices-are-falling/.

Etherington, Darrell. 2019. *Elon Musk tweets using SpaceX's Starlink satellite internet*. October 22. Accessed 2020.
https://techcrunch.com/2019/10/22/elon-musk-tweets-using-spacexs-starlink-satellite-internet/.

MAXIME, Samuel. 2019. *76 Ex-Prostitutes Graduate from Vocational Program.* August 26. Accessed October 2019.
https://sentinel.ht/post/news/community/11168-76-former-prostitutes-graduate-from-vocational-program.

United Nations. n.d. *Goal 5: Achieve gender equality and empower all women and girls*. Accessed 2019.
https://unstats.un.org/sdgs/report/2017/goal-05/.

CHAPTER 7

SARMIENTO, ISABELLA GOMEZ. 2019. *Congo's KOKOKO! Makes Joyful Dance Music From Instruments Made Of Junk*. October 19. Accessed 2019.
https://www.npr.org/sections/goatsandsoda/2019/10/19/766949887/congos-kokoko-makes-joyful-dance-music-from-instruments-made-of-junk?utm_medium=social&utm_source=twitter.com&utm_campaign=npr&utm_term=nprnews.

Psychology Today. n.d. *Big 5 Personality Traits*. Accessed 2019.
https://www.psychologytoday.com/intl/basics/big-5-personality-traits.

Godin, Seth. 2016. *Beware the gulf of disapproval*. May 27. Accessed 2019.
https://seths.blog/2016/05/beware-the-gulf-of-disapproval/.

Science, Association For Pyschological. 2015. *A Disagreeable Personality Can Help Get Original Ideas Noticed*. March 27. Accessed 2019.
https://www.psychologicalscience.org/news/minds-business/a-disagreeable-personality-can-help-get-original-ideas-noticed.html.

Frankl, Viktor. 1946. "Man's Search for Meaning." By Viktor Frankl, 136.

CHAPTER 8
IDEO. n.d. *What is Human-Centered Design?* Accessed 2019.
https://www.designkit.org/human-centered-design.

Vera Institute. 2016. *Participatory Action Research*. September 27. Accessed 2019.
https://www.youtube.com/watch?v=6D492AP9JP4&t=1s.

IDEO. n.d. *Brilliance by D-Rev*. Accessed 2019.
https://www.designkit.org/case-studies/5.

UBONGO KIDS. 2018. *Ubongo Kids Cartoons Help African Kids Develop Critical Skills For Success in a Rapidly Changing Future*. January 30. Accessed 2019.
https://afrinic.net/blog/317-ubongo-kids-cartoons-help-african-kids-develop-critical-skills-for-success-in-a-rapidly-changing-future.

CHAPTER 9
Bourguignon, François. 2015. *Revisiting the Debate on Inequality and Economic Development*. Revisiting the Debate on Inequality and Economic Development.

Ejiofor, Chiwetel. 2019. *The Boy Who Harnessed the Wind*. Directed by Chiwetel Ejiofor. Performed by Maxwell Simba.

Zetter, Kim. 2009. *Teen's DIY Energy Hacking Gives African Village New Hope*. February 10. Accessed 2019.
https://www.wired.com/2009/10/kamwamba-windmill/.

Duke University - The Fuqua School of Business. 2013. *The Pain of Paying: The Psychology of Money*. February 1st.
https://www.youtube.com/watch?v=PCujWv7Mc80.

BBC News. 2019. *Chile protests: Is inequality becoming worse?* October 21. Accessed Decembere 2019.
https://www.bbc.com/news/world-latin-america-50123494.

AJ+. 2019. *Haitian Teens Fight Plastic with Bamboo*. AJ+. June 10. Accessed 2019.
https://web.facebook.com/ajplusenglish/videos/haitian-teens-fight-plastic-with-bamboo/2343145872594643/?_rdc=1&_rdr.

Flecher, Jose. 2018. *Coutard Motors, une mine d'or ignorée*. October 31. Accessed 2019.
https://lenouvelliste.com/article/194539/coutard-motors-une-mine-dor-ignoree.

Wasti, Satish. 2018. *The Myth of Brain Drain: How Emigration Can Help Poor Countries*. October 16. Accessed 2019.
https://harvardpolitics.com/world/the-myth-of-brain-drain-how-emigration-can-help-poor-countries/.

Gibbs, Nancy. 2011. *To Fight Poverty, Invest in Girls.* February 14. Accessed 2019.
http://content.time.com/time/magazine/article/0,9171,2046045,00.html.

Caldbeck, Ryan. 2013. *Top Down Innovation Is Dead.* February 12. Accessed 2019.
https://www.forbes.com/sites/ryancaldbeck/2013/02/12/top-down-innovation-is-dead/#1f391ef724e1.

Koehn, Nancy. 2008. *The Time is Right for Creative Capitalism.* August 20. Accessed 2019.
https://hbswk.hbs.edu/item/the-time-is-right-for-creative-capitalism.

CUOFANO, GENNARO. n.d. *Brunello Cucinelli: The Humanistic Enterprise Business Model.* Accessed 2019.
https://fourweekmba.com/brunello-cucinelli-business-model/.

Worker Rights Consortium. 2013. *Stealing from the Poor: Wage Theft in the Haitian Apparel Industry.* Worker Rights Consortium .
https://www.workersrights.org/research-report/stealing-from-the-poor-wage-theft-in-the-haitian-apparel-industry/.

Wealyh X. 2019. *The Wealth-X Billionaire Census 2019.* May. Accessed 2019.
https://www.wealthx.com/report/the-wealth-x-billionaire-census-2019/.

CHAPTER 10

Ferris, Tim. 2018. "Catherine Hoke — The Master of Second Chances (#293)." *Tim Ferris Show* . January 21.
https://tim.blog/2018/01/21/catherine-hoke/.

Weill, Kelly. 2018. *Silicon Valley's Favorite Prison Reformer Accused of Sexual Assault and Harassment.* June 2018. Accessed 2019.
https://www.thedailybeast.com/silicon-valleys-favorite-prison-reformer-accused-of-sexual-assault-and-harassment?ref=home.

Roy, Aditi. 2017. *Defy Ventures helps inmates make the shift from prison to small business owners.* July 22. Accessed 2019.
https://www.cnbc.com/2017/07/22/defy-ventures-helps-inmates-make-the-shift-from-prison-to-small-business-owners.html.

Teddy. n.d. *Graduates.* Accessed 2019.
https://www.defyventures.org/our-community/graduates.

EDITORS, HISTORY.COM. 2010. *Bermuda Triangle.* October 7. Accessed 2019 .
https://www.history.com/topics/folklore/bermuda-triangle.

Clear, James. n.d. *Motivation is Overvalued. Environment Often Matters More.* Accessed 2018.
https://jamesclear.com/power-of-environment.

APA Dictionary of Psychology Search. n.d. Accessed 2019.
https://dictionary.apa.org/eustress.

WeThrive. n.d. *WeThrive.* Accessed 2019.
http://teamwethrive.org/about/.

CHAPTER 11
Let's Give A Damn Podcast. 2018. *Daquan Oliver — WeThrive Helps Youth Build Real Companies And Participate In Tomorrow's Economy.* Nick Laparra. December 11. Accessed 2019.
https://anchor.fm/letsgiveadamn/episodes/Daquan-Oliver--WeThrive-Helps-Youth-Build-Real-Companies-And-Participate-In-Tomorrows-Economy-e3is1t.

Goode, Robin White. 2018. *WETHRIVE PUTS YOUTH ON PATH TO OPPORTUNITY.* March 18. Accessed 2019.
https://www.blackenterprise.com/wethrive-helps-youth-beat-path-opportunity/.

WeThrive. n.d. *Daquan J. Oliver.* Accessed 2019.
http://teamwethrive.org/founding/.

blackvegansrock.com/. n.d. *FEATURE: Nzingah Oniwosan.* Accessed 2019.
http://www.blackvegansrock.com/blog/2017/11/1/feature-nzingah-oniwosan.

magazine.pellealvegetale.it. n.d. *The Brunello Cucinelli's humanistic capitalism.* Accessed 2019.
http://magazine.pellealvegetale.it/en/humanistic-capitalism-brunello-cucinelli/.

Mead, Rebecca. 2010. *THE PRINCE OF SOLOMEO.* March 22. Accessed 2019.
https://www.newyorker.com/magazine/2010/03/29/the-prince-of-solomeo.

Bilyeu, Tom. 2017. *A Lesson in Millennial Entrepreneurship | Gerard Adams on Impact Theory.* June 27. Accessed 2019.
https://www.youtube.com/watch?v=TRY-aPC1MUs.

n.d. *About Gerard.* Accessed 2019.
https://gerardadams.com/about/.

Hunckler, Matt. 2017. *FOWNDERS GUIDE TO MILLENNIAL MOTIVATION AND AUDIENCE BUILDING WITH ELITE DAILY CO-FOUNDER.* May 9. Accessed 2019.
https://powderkeg.com/fownders-guide-millennial-motivation-audience-building-elite-daily-co-founder/.

Shontell, Alyson. 2014. *How Three 20-Somethings Built Elite Daily, A Site With 40 Million Readers, With $60,000.* June 13. Accessed 2019.
https://www.businessinsider.com/elite-daily-raises-15-million-and-has-40-million-uniques-2014-6.

Fry, Chris. 2017. *Gomes Group And Fownders Bringing Housing, Work Space, And Biergarten To Newark's Emerging Silicon City.* April 27. Accessed 2019.
https://jerseydigs.com/gomes-group-fownders-building-out-newarks-emerging-silicon-city/.

CHAPTER 12
Josceline Anne Mascarenhas. 2018. *The Man Who Moved a Mountain.* October 9. Accessed 2019.
http://www.dailygood.org/story/2103/the-man-who-moved-a-mountain/.

Ventures, Skyland. 2015. *Manjhi — The man who moved a mountain — literally.* November 25. Accessed 2019.
https://medium.com/@Genius50/manjhi-the-man-who-moved-a-mountain-literally-363d38ea2492.

Robinson, Sir Ken. 2016. *Does School Kill Creativity?* February. Accessed 2019. https://www.ted.com/talks/sir_ken_robinson_do_schools_kill_creativity?language=en.

Quartz. 2019. *Quartz Africa Innovators 2019: leading the change for Africa's future.* September. Accessed 2019. https://qz.com/africa/1700312/quartz-africa-innovators-2019/.

GLANTON, DAHLEEN. 2017. *Growing up with poverty and violence: A North Lawndale teen's story.* March 10. Accessed 2019. https://www.chicagotribune.com/columns/dahleen-glanton/ct-poverty-violence-glanton-met-20170309-column.html.

Kenny, Charles. 2017. *Stop blaming poor countries' poverty on corruption—sometimes it's just bad luck.* August 1. Accessed 2019. https://qz.com/1024546/stop-blaming-poor-countries-poverty-on-corruption-sometimes-its-just-bad-luck/.

HARFORD, TIM. 2012. *ADAPT.* Picador Paper.

—. 2012. *ADAPT.* Picador Paper.

Bornstein, David. 2007. *How to Change the World: Social Entrepreneurs and the Power of New Ideas, Updated Edition.* Oxford University Press, U.S.A.

Mary J Cronin, Mary J. Cronin. 2014. *Top Down Innovation (SpringerBriefs in Business).* Springer.

HISTORY.COM EDITORS. 2009. *Napoleon Bonaparte.* November 9. Accessed February 2020. https://www.history.com/topics/france/napoleon.

Stewart, Lauren. 2019. *The High Cost of Low Wages in Haiti.* Solidarity Center.

Made in the USA
Monee, IL
22 March 2021